Campfire

COMPANION

MQ Publications Limited
12 The Ivories, 6–8 Northampton Street
London N1 2HY
Tel: +44 (0) 20 7359 2244
Fax: +44 (0) 20 7359 1616
email: mail@mqpublications.com
www.mqpublications.com

ISBN: 1-84072-778-0

10 9 8 7 6 5 4 3 2 1

Printed and bound in China

Campfire

COMPANION

DAVID BAIRD

MQP

Contents

Introduction

When we sit around a campfire and stare deep into its flames we become part of a chain that links us back to the very first moment man discovered he could create and control fire. The flickering of flames instantly transports you back to the pioneering days of frontiersmen, memories of childhood in the Boy Scouts or Girl Guides, or family camping vacations where everything looked, smelled, and tasted wonderful. Campfires conjure up images of cowboys and coffee pots, Dutch ovens and slow cooking stews, ballads, storytelling, and nights out under the stars.

Campfire Companion contains a wealth of historical, practical, and fascinating material. Follow the step-by-step projects—fending for yourself in the wilderness is so satisfying, and with a little help from this book, you'll discover that your capabilities far outreach anything you ever imagined.

The campfire is the traditional heart of the camp—a place where like-minded campers can congregate at the end of the day, warm themselves, and listen to other's tales of adventure. There really is something for everyone in this treasured collection—the perfect companion for any camping vacation. Pull it out of your backpack and share evocative literary extracts on the joys of the campfire, amusing quotes and insights, or strike up a rousing traditional scouting song with your fellow campers, while sharing the fire's warmth. Come and join us around the campfire.

"One of the pleasantest times of camping out is the period immediately after supper, when the hunters lie in the blaze of the fire-light, talking over what they have done during the day and making their plans for the morrow. And how soundly a man who has worked hard sleeps in the open, none but he who has tried it knows."

THEODORE ROOSEVELT
Hunting Trips of a Ranchman

MW00490877

Flicker of the Campfire

(SUNG AT CAMPFIRE PROGRAMS)

The flicker of the campfire
The wind in the pines:
The stars in the heavens,
A moon that shines,
A place where people gather,
Make friends of all kinds,
A place where all men's troubles
Are always left behind.
So give me the light of the campfire
Warm and bright
And give me some friends to sing with
I'll be here all night
Love is for those who find it
I've found mine right here,
Just you and me and the campfire
And songs we love to hear.

Dear Mom

We are having a great time up here in the mountains. Our scoutmaster told us all to write our parents, in case you saw the flood on television and got worried about us. We're OK and only one of the tents got washed away, but that had been ripped by the bears anyway so it didn't much matter. The flood missed us because we were all halfway up the mountain looking for Roger, who went missing two days ago. That reminds me, can you please telephone Roger's parents and tell them he's OK, and he'll write as soon as his arm's out of the splint. It was good fun riding in the mountain-rescue vehicle and it was lucky that there was so much forked lightning to see by or we might never have found poor Roger. The scoutmaster was pretty angry at Roger for not telling him he was going hiking alone, but Roger swears he did tell him but that he probably didn't hear because he was treating George for snakebite at the time.

We had to go out on our own and make campfires. Did you know that if you pour gasoline on a fire the can will blow up? George does now. Pity about losing a second tent in the flames. Hey Mom, eyebrows do grow back, don't they?

The scoutmaster says we should be back by Friday, if he can get the van repaired after rolling it down the hill. (Don't worry, we all crawled out unhurt.) The brakes had been pretty good up until then. Anyway, he said we've got to be ☞

prepared with a vehicle that old, you have to expect something to go wrong—I think that's why he can't get it insured. It has big bumpers though, and we rode on them the last ten miles to keep cool. That's how we knew the brakes were OK, because when the scoutmaster did an emergency stop, Mike shot off and landed in a bush. Then we all took turns to drive when we got onto the mountain track. Don't worry, there's no other cars up here, just logging trucks.

Anyway, today the guys were down by the dark water diving off the rocks, but I had to keep an eye on Roger. The scoutmaster said that if we were careful not to destroy another canoe by going over the waterfall, we could paddle around the lake, which was great fun and much easier without life jackets on since they all got washed away. The water level has gone down a lot since the flood, and you can see the treetops again now.

When we arrived back at camp, we got a chance to practice for our first-aid merit badges after Simon cut his leg diving off the rocks. Have you ever used a tourniquet, Mom?

We had chicken for lunch, cooked over our campfire and it tasted pretty good. It wasn't burnt at all. It was nice and pink and juicy and lukewarm. But in all the excitement, everybody started throwing up after lunch. Scoutmaster said not to worry, that it was probably just food poisoning. He told us that they used to get it a lot when he was in prison. Anyway, I've gotta go. We're going to the village to mail these letters and buy some bullets.

So don't worry about us OK? We're all having a swell time.

Your loving son

P.S. Have I ever had a tetanus shot?

Scout Vespers

THE BOY SCOUT SONGBOOK, 1963

Softly falls the light of day,
While our campfire fades away.
Silently each Scout should ask
Have I done my daily task?
Have I kept my honor bright?
Can I guiltless sleep tonight?
Have I done and have I dared
Everything to be prepared?

"Hello Mudda, Hello Fadda
Here I am at Camp Granada."

ALLAN SHERMAN

Breakfast Tortillas

6 small, dry, corn tortillas
oil, for deep-frying
1 onion, finely chopped
8oz/225g leftover cooked beef, pork,
    or ham, cut into bite-sized pieces
3/4 cup/6oz/150g mild cheddar cheese,
    shredded

1. Chop or tear the tortillas into bite-sized pieces. Heat about 2 inches of oil in a skillet over medium to high heat until a piece of tortilla dropped in the oil turns golden and crisp in a few seconds. Fry the pieces of tortilla in batches until nicely golden all over, removing and draining on paper towels as they are cooked.

2. Pour off all but a little oil from the skillet and fry the onion in the remaining oil over a low heat, stirring from time to time, until just beginning to color.

3. Add the meat and cook gently, stirring, until warmed through, 1 to 2 minutes.

4. Stir in the tortilla pieces and half the cheese, then sprinkle the top with the remaining cheese. Cover the pan and place over a low heat for a few minutes until the cheese has melted. With the tortillas, cooked meat, and cheese, you may not need any added seasoning.

You can, of course, use ready-made tortilla chips for ease. Stirring in 2 or 3 beaten eggs will turn it into something resembling a Spanish omelet type of tortilla.

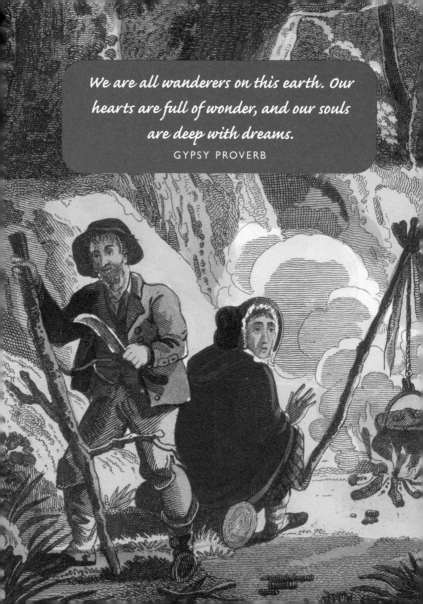

We are all wanderers on this earth. Our hearts are full of wonder, and our souls are deep with dreams.

GYPSY PROVERB

Life Around the Campfire

Gypsies are believed to have migrated from the Indus Valley in northern India in the ninth century, traveling through Persia, and reaching eastern Europe about one thousand years ago. And they have continued to travel ever since, which perhaps explains their language—a rich mix of Sanskrit, Greek, and Romanian, among others. The earliest record of Gypsies as musicians is a Persian reference to a group of *luri*, a caste of musicians and dancers, who had come from India around 420 B.C. to perform in front of the Persian king. Their need to travel is not just a whim; it goes back a very long way. One of the main reasons for conflict between the Gypsy community and other members of society is that many do not recognize the Gypsies need or right to a nomadic way of life.

A stereotyped view of Gypsies is often a very romanticized image of travelers, living in prettily painted wagons, or Gypsy women wearing large gold hoop earrings, dancing wildly around a campfire, and shaking a tambourine to elaborate songs played on the fiddle or flamenco guitar. Some even see them (however unfairly), as lawless, rebellious, and lazy. However, there are a great many things about the Gypsy lifestyle and traditions that other people do not understand. There have always been, and still are, strict codes of hygiene and behavior that Gypsies adhere to. They also follow a strong work ethic.

The Gypsies have always tended to make their camps away from disturbances and non-Gypsies. They gravitate toward remote areas, chosen for their proximity to water and firewood. But they also are drawn to areas where there might be the opportunity to earn some money by providing labor or selling goods. In England, they would traditionally follow the seasons to go hop-picking in Kent, apple-picking in the orchards of Essex, soft-fruit-picking in the height of summer in the Fens, and many would take on the back-breaking work of hoeing and picking potatoes. Some Gypsies would breed and sell pets; others would sell flowers or lace. And of course, Gypsies are most well known for telling people's fortunes, if their palms are crossed with silver. They have always been close-knit communities, whose inhabitants are good at making do, while regularly being harassed by authorities to pack up and be on their way again. Wherever you go in the world and encounter Gypsies, the story is very much the same.

Gypsies are safety conscious, and once a camp is located, they explore the area to identify any potential dangers that might exist, such as disused mineshafts or unsafe water. In the early nineteenth century, Gypsies didn't have the beautiful wagons that we associate them with today and would live wherever they could. They moved into abandoned shacks and caves or built "bender tents," which were ☞

like the covered wagons used by cowboys, but without the wagon. The benders were semirounded with a wooden, ribbed interior skeleton covered with animal hide, or waterproof material, secured to the ground. These were easily constructed and extremely portable, making them perfect for the traveling way of life. They were also fairly spacious and comfortable to dwell in, as well as providing good shelter from bad weather.

About halfway through the nineteenth century, the horse-drawn wagons, known as vardoes, became the popular mode

of travel, providing good transportation and accommodation all under one roof. Their interior was elaborate and highly practical and the Gypsy code called for a traditionally high degree of cleanliness.

In 1840, Charles Dickens provided an excellent description of Mrs. Jarley's van with its bed, stove, closet, and several chests, in his book *The Old Curiosity Shop*:

"One half of it…was carpeted, and so partitioned off at the further end as to accommodate a sleeping place, constructed after the fashion of a berth on board ship, which was shaded, like the windows, with fair white curtains.…The other half served for a kitchen, and was fitted up with a stove whose small chimney passed through the roof. It also held a closet or larder, several chests, a great pitcher of water, and a few cooking utensils and articles of crockery. These latter necessaries hung upon the walls, which in that portion of the establishment devoted to the lady of the caravan, were ornamented with such gayer and lighter decorations as a triangle and a couple of well-thumbed tambourines."

What Dickens describes here was probably the Reading Wagon or the old type of Gypsy vardo. These types of wagons had large wheels running outside the body of the van, which sloped steeply outward toward the eaves and curved roof. ☞

Today, the modern Romani relies more on the car, as traditional places of work have grown farther apart and greater areas must be covered in a much shorter time. Consequently, the vardo has given way to gleaming caravans with all the comforts you could wish for inside.

A Gypsy wedding is an important event. The festivities can go on for days with great feasting and celebration. There is very often an open fire for roasting food over for the wedding party. A favorite dish on these occasions used to be roasted hedgehog. Before the groom can take the bride home, she is abducted by her unmarried friends who surround her, walling her in, and the groom out. The groom is eventually allowed to break through the unmarried friends and reclaim his bride. The bride's mother-in-law then helps the new bride to make a knot in her handkerchief, which she is never again seen in public without. Once married, the bride will leave her family to live with her husband's family, and it is not until the birth of their first child that they will be able to move into their own home.

Sometimes Gypsies will permit an outsider, or *gaje* to be adopted into their clan. Firstly, the outsider must prove themselves worthy to the rest of the clan by drinking a special potion from the magical Gypsy cup at a ceremony. Those who do so will have their blood changed to Gypsy blood.

Camp Coffee

Can you smell it? Camp life wouldn't be the same without a morning brew of fresh coffee over an open fire. Load a coffee pot with a handful of roughly ground coffee beans, a few eggshells for body, and a quart of clear springwater collected from a nearby mountain spring. There are tales of people who forgot their coffee pots at home and in desperation turned to bait cans, or a child's tin potty. One poor desperado even attempted to brew coffee in a hiking boot.

Coffee, Cowboy-Style

MAKES 8 CUPS

> 7 tbsp/3 ½ oz/100g ground
>   roast coffee
> crushed shell of 1 egg

1. Bring 8 cups/2 liters of water to a boil.
2. Put the coffee and eggshell in a bag and work to mix well. If you are grinding your own beans at home, add the eggshell at the end and pulse to mix.
3. Put the coffee and eggshell mixture into a coffee pot and pour in the boiling water. Simmer for 4 minutes, add a half-cup of cold water, and serve.

Chuck Wagon Etiquette

The practicalities of a cattle drive meant that in order to eat well, cowboys had to hire a good, reliable, often older cowboy who had done his share of range work, and who could be depended on to drive the chuck wagon and all its supplies. The cook was considered the "Old Lady" of the trail drive and had many nicknames, including cookie, biscuit shooter, bean burner, or sourdough, to name a few. The chuck wagon became his responsibility, as it was the center of the cowboys' working and social lives. It was a larder, a kitchen, and a supply wagon all in one, and without it the long cattle drives into the North would have been near impossible. More often than not the cook would be better paid than the other cowboys, as so much depended on him.

Often the youngest in the camp was assigned as his helper, sometimes prescribed with a girl's name such as "Little Mary." For these helpers, the great day would eventually come when they could go out and ride as an equal to the rest and without their kitchen name!

Cowboys always ride downwind of the chuck wagon to keep from getting dust in the supplies and never ride their horses through the kitchen area. They are strictly forbidden to eat at the chuck wagon table. Any cowboy refilling their coffee cup is obliged to serve refills to others if a member of his outfit yells "Man at the pot."

Beach Parties

There's nothing like cooking your food over a campfire while listening to the crashing of waves on the shore and setting up camp on the beach is one of the most old-fashioned, romantic ways to sleep out under the stars. The relaxed, vacation atmosphere of a beach campsite makes it the perfect place to hold an impromptu party.

The entire notion of holding a party on the beach actually stemmed from other more practical reasons for having campfires on beaches. Fishermen would return with their catch and cook it fresh by the sea. And marooned sailors would sit by the breakers burning their beacon in the hope of being spotted by passing ships in the night.

The American tradition of holding clambakes on the beach dates back to precolonial times, when the native peoples of the New England area gathered food from the beach. They would dig out large pits in the sand, put in a layer of heated rocks, and cover the rocks with seaweed. This would produce steam that would cook their food. Early settlers continued this tradition and it has been popular ever since. Choose your favorite shellfish and crustaceans, such as clams, lobster, mussels, or shrimp for a seafood feast. Many like to serve their shellfish with potatoes, onions, and corn on the cob—wholesome accompaniments for a cool, late summer's evening.

Scout Jamboree

It wasn't long after the start of scouting in 1908 that the movement rapidly spread across the world. This gave Baden-Powell the idea of bringing scouts of all nationalities together somehow, in some form of organized camp. Unfortunately, in 1914 his plans came to an abrupt halt with the outbreak of World War I. All plans were put on hold until the world situation changed and circumstances would permit a proper Imperial and International Jamboree to be held. As the war ended in 1918, it was decided that the Jamboree should take place in London, England, two years later.

So with the horrors of World War I placed firmly in the past, the very first World Jamboree was held at Olympia, in London, back in 1920. There were 8,000 scouts present, from 34 countries under a huge glass-roofed building that was turned into a camp. The floor was covered with earth and turf for pitching tents, and competitions and events were held every day. There were so many scouts they couldn't be accommodated under the one roof, so some scouts camped out in the deer park at Richmond, nearby. There was an alligator brought from Florida, a baby crocodile from Jamaica, a lioness cub from Rhodesia (now Zimbabwe), a number of monkeys from South Africa, a baby elephant, and a camel. In a demonstration of international goodwill, Baden-Powell was acknowledged by the scouts to be the Chief Scout of the World in an impromptu ceremony toward the close of the Jamboree. The tribute so moved Baden-Powell that at the closing ceremony he gave this parting message:

> "Brother Scouts, differences exist between the peoples of the world in thought and sentiment, just as they do in language and physique. The Jamboree has taught us that if we exercise mutual forbearance and give and take, then there is sympathy and harmony if it be your will. Let us go forth fully determined that we will develop among ourselves and our boys that comradeship, through the worldwide spirit of the scout brotherhood, so that we may help to develop peace and happiness in the world and goodwill among men."

In 1937, the year of the fifth World Jamboree in Heldin Vogelensang-Bloemendaal, Netherlands (see image on pages 38–39) there were a total of 28,750 scouts present from 54 countries and a total of 120 showers and 650 water faucets had to be installed. Daily displays were held. The Girl Guides also used the arena to welcome Lady Baden-Powell, World Chief Guide. Lord Baden-Powell was 80 years old at this time and was presented with the Jamboree emblem, a Jacob staff.

ÊTRE PRÊT

"The most important object in Boy Scout training is to educate, not instruct."

SIR ROBERT BADEN-POWELL

Campfire Wood

HOW TO CHOOSE AND GATHER THE BEST WOOD AND HOW TO MAKE A WOODPILE

When it comes to the campfire, preparation is vital. Always make sure that there are sufficient quantities of tinder, kindling, and fuel available to ignite the fire and sustain it through the night. Nobody wants to walk out into the pitch darkness in search of firewood.

Tinder is any material that will catch fire using the minimum of heat. Really good tinder needs only a spark to get it going. In the wild, look for bird down, dried grasses, some fine dry wood shavings, birch bark, dried powdered fungi, or dried pine needles. In an emergency survival situation, a piece of waxed paper or even the lint from cotton clothing would work. The downy inside of abandoned birds nests is useful, as are powdery bird and bat droppings. Make absolutely certain that whatever you try to use is absolutely dry. It's best to take enough with you to get you going, and always be on the lookout for good tinder, collecting it as you see it while camping.

For kindling use wood that will catch fire relatively easily and that will produce enough heat to burn larger, less combustible materials and keep them alight. Collect small dry twigs and softer woods, particularly those that produce resins as these catch light very quickly and burn hot. Kindling produces quite a lot of sparks so be careful they don't set anything else alight. Kindling found on the ground is likely to be damp, so search for standing deadwood instead. A helpful tip is to use a sharp knife to feather kindling sticks by making a series of shallow cuts in them.

Finally, add the fuel. First use dry wood that has been collected from standing dead trees. This will ignite quickly and provide enough heat to burn greener wood, if you need to. It will also give you time to dry other wood beside the fire, and can later be used for fuel. Softwoods, such as cedar, hemlock, pine, spruce, willow, and chestnut burn quite fast, tend to give out a lot of sparks, and need tending to through the night. Hickory, oak, or beech mixed with a bit of green wood will provide a long-lasting fire with lots of hot coals. It also gives off just enough smoke to keep the bugs at bay.

Many people advocate circling the fire with stones or rocks, but this can sometimes be dangerous. Rocks that have been under water for some time can contain a large amount of moisture. Once the water inside them heats up they can turn into grenades. The water heats and expands faster than the rock and they can explode, sending dangerous fragments flying everywhere.

It is important to choose and prepare your fireplace carefully. It should be sheltered from the possibility of ☞

☞ high winds but never lit at the base of a tree or stump. Always clear away any twigs, leaves, moss, dry grass, and other combustible materials a good six-foot circle away from the fire. (If you must dig turf, lift it carefully, and pile it away from the fire. Keep it dampened so you can replace it later.) A clear, dry earth base is what is needed.

If you are forced to camp where there is no possibility of dry ground, you will have to create a raised platform or temple fire of green wood by using four uprights with forks midway along their length at not less than 12 inches from the ground level. Rest a horizontal square frame of four pieces of green wood in the forks so that if you rest a layer of thicker green logs across this you will have a platform 12 or more inches above the wet ground or snow. Over the rested logs, lay several inches of earth or, use rocks. (Make sure that you have previously knocked the rocks together to test that they are not dangerously porous, hollow sounding, or flaky.) The platform that has been created is where you will prepare your campfire.

Lay a bed of good, dry tinder and around it build a tepee shape using kindling sticks. Ignite the tinder, and once the kindling has really caught alight, you can gradually start adding larger sticks until the entire thing is burning steadily and is hot enough to take your good fuel logs.

Tall Tales

There is an art to telling an engaging and entertaining campfire story—it's a wonderful way to bond with your fellow campers and helps to create a special ambience around the fire. Fill your story with atmosphere and dynamics that are guaranteed to have listeners glued to the edge of their seats. It's best if there's a sudden shock somewhere in the story to stand their hairs on end.

Rehearse your campfire story until you know it well and are confident of how you will deliver it when the time arrives. Think about giving it the right dramatic flow, and remember to raise the dynamics just at the precise moment to obtain the desired reaction from listeners. Why not make your friends jump with an explosive noise—everyone loves to be scared once in a while! Try and keep your voice hushed and low, so that your audience has to lean in close to hear your terrible tale.

An effective, well-told yarn can be performed anywhere and still have a great impact, but a forest setting at night or a camp that is beside a still lake will add a great deal to the atmosphere of your story. Imagine telling a tale of a creature that rises from the still waters while being assembled around your lakeside campfire, or enjoy your audience's reaction when you tell them about the ghostly bear that haunts the forest that you are camping in!

How to Make Kitchen Equipment

Create yourself a comfortable and functional campsite kitchen by working at a few simple camp crafts.

PATROL TABLE

Here's how to make a camp table, also sometimes known as a patrol table. Start by selecting two medium-sized trees that are near each other, about 6ft/1.8m apart.

Select two poles that can bridge this distance to the outside edge of each tree and then lash them to the tree at table height. Once this has been done, other poles can be used to fill in the gap between the two lashed poles, and these can either be lashed or wedged into place. At the end of this process, you will have a good working surface.

Next, select four sturdy branches that have forked ends and drive them into the ground on the outside of each tree to a height of about 30in/76cm with the forks pointing up to the sky. On these forks, rest one pole to each two forks, which will create an H shape with the work surface, if you

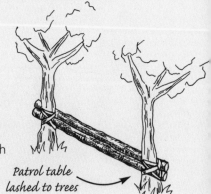

Patrol table lashed to trees

were looking down from above. Bind these poles to the forks then between them, resting on them and running parallel to the working surface, but at the lower height you have set the forks at, rest a couple of sturdy poles either side. These are the benches and when positioned correctly they can be bound to the frame, so that by the end of the process you will have created a structure that is similar to a picnic table. Here you can eat, look at maps, play cards or board games, and have camp meetings. ☞

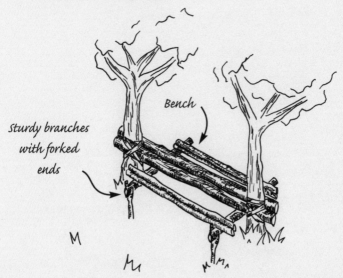

Bench

sturdy branches with forked ends

COOKING FRAME

Ideally, when cooking over a campfire the pot should be kept at a height that is above the hot coals and flames. Construct a simple frame that will control the pot's height.

Find a branch that is about 24in/61cm long with a fork at one end, and drive it into the ground near the campfire but not near enough to catch alight (you can adjust things as you go along). Find another longer stick that can rest in the fork and position it so it holds the pot over the fire, with the other end driven into the earth and held safely in place with some rocks. This will prevent your camp stew from falling into the fire. It's wise to cut a small notch near the cooking end of the stick to help prevent any pots from slipping off. Tie the pot handle to the stick, just to be safe!

Rocks to hold stick

Pot of campfire stew

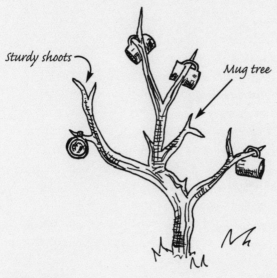

sturdy shoots

Mug tree

MUG TREE

Make a mug tree for your campsite kitchen area, where mugs can be hung to dry after being rinsed and will remain dirt-free. Take a walk in the woods and search for a suitable fallen branch that has a number of sturdy shoots coming from it. Using a sharp camping knife, cut these shoots back to a series of small forks (long enough for mug handles or long enough to slip the vessel onto entirely if your cups don't have handles). Find a good place in camp that is out of the way and drive the mug tree into the ground securely, then decorate it with mugs or beakers. ☞

BROOM

It's best to have a broom at hand to sweep away excess leaves when making a fire, or to get rid of food debris so as not to attract bugs or larger animals.

Make yourself a traditional besom broom. Find a sturdy central stick about the same thickness as a broomstick and gather a bundle of whip-thin twigs about 30in/76cm long. Trim these so that they are all the same length, and then bind them onto the stick, leaving half the length unbound below the stick to sweep with and the rest securely bound to it. Tidy up after yourself and sweep all debris into the campfire to incinerate.

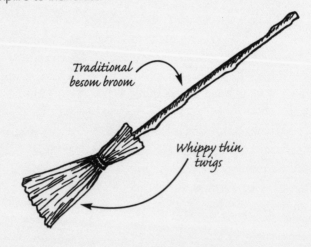

Traditional besom broom

Whippy thin twigs

PLATE RACK

Create a simple plate rack. Its length will depend on how many plates are in use, but it's so quick and simple you can be quite telescopic with the materials!

Run two fairly straight sticks along the ground to form the tramline for the plates to sit across, and then drive into the ground outside of the two long sticks, smaller lengths of stick in parallel pairs along the length. Add another pair of sticks for every plate you wish to include.

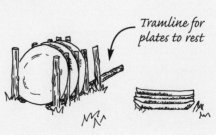

Tramline for plates to rest

DISH MOP

Washing up can be made simpler by making a useful dish mop.

Strips of rag or cloth

Short stubby stick

As with the besom broom, take a a short stubby stick a few inches long, and bind onto it some strips of rag or find a slightly longer stubby stick that you can mash the end with using a rock to free the fibers until it is quite bushy. ☞

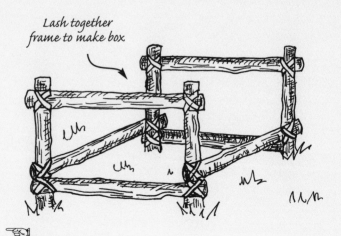

Lash together frame to make box

FIREWOOD BOX

Firewood left strewn around the campsite is asking for an accident to happen and nobody wants to trip over into the campfire or twist their ankle. A log box with a simple framework will prevent this. It will also keep your wood off the damp ground and you can keep an eye on how much needs replacing as the evening passes.

Drive two poles parallel into the ground and lash a crossbar onto them and repeat the process a couple of feet away from this so it resembles two goals on a soccer field. Now bind another crossbar to every pole several inches above the ground and rest some longer poles between the two "goals" on the lower crossbars, on which firewood can be piled and rested.

WASH BASIN

Finally make a 4ft/1.4m high tripod of sticks, lashing them at the center and tying them off at the legs so the top splays enough to place a plastic basin in and you will have the ideal wash basin for doing the dishes in or washing your face in. (An optional shelf can be slotted in to rest your dish mop or soap.)

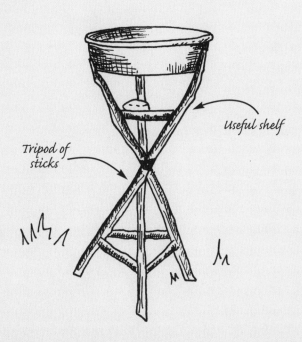

Useful shelf

Tripod of
sticks

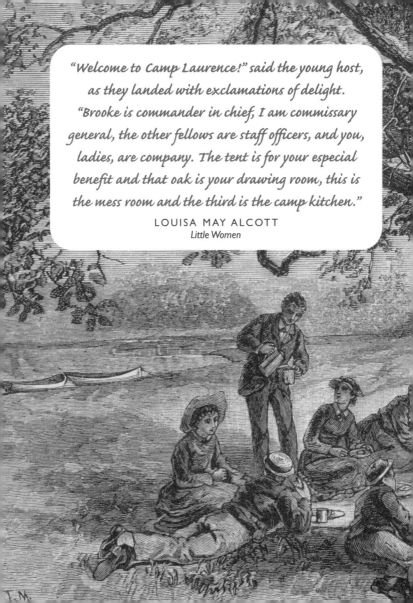

"Welcome to Camp Laurence!" said the young host, as they landed with exclamations of delight. "Brooke is commander in chief, I am commissary general, the other fellows are staff officers, and you, ladies, are company. The tent is for your especial benefit and that oak is your drawing room, this is the mess room and the third is the camp kitchen."

LOUISA MAY ALCOTT
Little Women

Little Women

by

LOUISA MAY ALCOTT

Jo, feeling that her late lessons in cookery were to do her honor, went to preside over the coffeepot, while the children collected dry sticks, and the boys made a fire and got water from a spring near by. Miss Kate sketched and Frank talked to Beth, who was making little mats of braided rushes to serve as plates.

The commander in chief and his aides soon spread the table-cloth with an inviting array of eatables and drinkables, prettily decorated with green leaves. Jo announced that the coffee was ready, and everyone settled themselves to a hearty meal, for youth is seldom dyspeptic, and exercise develops wholesome appetites. A very merry lunch it was, for everything seemed fresh and funny, and frequent peals of laughter startled a venerable horse who fed near by. There was a pleasing inequality in the table, which produced many mishaps to cups and plates, acorns dropped in the milk, little black ants partook of the refreshments without being invited, and fuzzy caterpillars swung down from the tree to see what was going on. Three white-headed children peeped over the fence, and an objectionable dog barked at them from the other side of the river with all his might and main.

"There's salt here," said Laurie, as he handed Jo a saucer of berries.

"Thank you, I prefer spiders," she replied, fishing up two unwary little ones who had gone to a creamy death. "How dare you remind me of that horrid dinner party, when yours is so nice in every way?" added Jo, as they both laughed and ate out of one plate, the china having run short.

"I had an uncommonly good time that day, and haven't got over it yet. This is no credit to me, you know, I don't do anything. It's you and Meg and Brooke who make it all go, and I'm no end obliged to you. What shall we do when we can't eat anymore?" asked Laurie, feeling that his trump card had been played when lunch was over.

On Top of Spaghetti

(TRY SINGING TO THE TUNE OF "OLD SMOKEY")

On top of Spaghetti, all covered with cheese,
I lost my poor meatball when somebody sneezed.

It rolled off the table, and onto the floor,
And then my poor meatball rolled right out the door.

It rolled down the garden, and under a bush,
And then my poor meatball was nothing but mush!

The mush was as tasty, as tasty could be,
And the very next summer it grew into a tree.

The tree was all covered, all covered with moss,
And on it grew meatballs, all covered with sauce.

So if you have spaghetti, all covered with cheese,
Hold onto your meatball, 'cause someone might sneeze.

Denominational Camps

By far the most popular type of camp with countless millions of people enjoying them worldwide annually, are the denominational camps. Set up to help campers develop a love for the outdoors, it's an environment where members are encouraged to unleash their creativity and nurture their own self-esteem and respect for others in a supportive environment.

These types of camps are more popular today than at any other time. This is possibly because when they first started out, people were suspicious and worried that these camps were going to isolate campers from the real world and brainwash them into some kind of fundamentalist way of thinking. Nothing could have been further from the truth.

Nowadays if you attend a denominational camp, you're more likely to spend your day top-roping; rappeling; bouldering; hiking in amazing valleys; swimming in crystal clear lakes and rivers; exploring rock pools and water caves; or shooting the rapids on rubber rafts. You may get to experience a taste of another way of life—perhaps sleep in authentic Sioux tepee, learn archery, attend evening campfires, and eat different kinds of foods. Whatever the season, these camps see the world as God's playground. Whether it is swimming, canoeing, sailing, sports, archery, throwing horseshoes, fishing, campfire circles, challenge courses, exploring the wide-open spaces, hiking trails, pony trekking, or mountain biking—the camps are designed to stretch the mind, body, and spirit with adventurous play in the playground of creation. It's a great way to enable self-discovery and personal growth. Denominational camps can instill special feelings of pride about faith, heritage, and traditions while at the same time helping campers to develop an understanding and a love for the outdoors, nature, and the environment.

Denominational camps won't twist your arm and try to involve you in something you don't want a part of. Usually, if you want it, those who run these camps will have available some form of theme-oriented program, campfire talks, and devotions, often at no extra cost, and at your request. However, you're more likely to come away with a qualification as a white-water rafting guide or a climbing instructor and you will have built some meaningful relationships, getting in touch with yourself and the world you live in.

Summers of great adventures translate into a lifetime of wonderful memories, and denominational camps are the ideal place to build lasting and worthwhile relationships, particularly with yourself, the world around you, and your beliefs. Surrounded by majestic scenery and beautiful lakes, it's awe-inspiring and refreshing to immerse yourself in the wilderness and to truly get in touch with nature in the company of like-minded campers.

Corn Chowder

SERVES 6–8

½ lb/225g salt pork or thick-cut
   fatty bacon, finely diced
1 large onion, chopped
2-3 celery stalks, chopped (optional)
½ lb/200g potatoes, diced
1 dried bay leaf
pinch of paprika (optional)
3 tbsp flour
1½ cups/450ml milk
2 cups/450g (approx. 4 medium
   cobs)freshly scraped corn or one
   15-oz can corn, drained

Cooking the corn first on a fire or barbecue will give the soup an extra full, delicious flavor. If no fresh milk is available, diluted evaporated milk can be used, or the potatoes mashed to give a creamy texture before adding the corn.

1. In a large Dutch oven, fry the pork or bacon until golden brown and the fat has run. Add the onion and celery and sauté until softened.

2. Add the potatoes with 2 cups of water, the bay leaf, paprika if using, and seasoning to taste. Bring to a boil, then lower the heat and simmer until the potatoes are soft, about 15 to 20 minutes.

3. Mix the flour with about one-quarter of the milk. Add to the pot and stir until well blended. Simmer for about 5 minutes. At the same time, heat the rest of the milk in a separate pan.

4. Add the hot milk and corn to the soup and warm through gently, but don't allow to boil. Adjust the seasoning and remove the bay leaf before serving.

You can give this a modern lift by adding some diced red pepper with the potatoes and a good handful of chopped cilantro with the corn.

The Modern Camper

Well, we've done it. We've survived millennium after millennium and reached a stage of sophistication so advanced that we can send vehicles to Mars and TV pictures back from it. We can clone a sheep, shop on the Internet, and someone has even designed clothing with built-in bacteria that will actually eat dirt so that clothes remain permanently clean. We commute more than ever before, and every waking hour of every day is filled with noise, pollution, chaos, and demands. So what better way to get away from it all than to take yourself and your family camping for the weekend, where the air is clean and everything is good for you.

We don't need the old tent and the fishing poles from our youth. Not us—we're modern campers. Time is money. We've got the RV now. It cost us twice what our house did and it has curtains and carpets throughout. The refrigerator is big enough for a 12-person Thanksgiving turkey, three six-packs of beer, and ten quarts of ice cream (we don't like to overdo it). We used to worry about the rain spoiling our camping trips, but now we've got DVD and satellite TV, five-in-one digital surround sound, and a fold-down plasma screen. All we have to do is go online on our laptop Bluetooth firewire computer and send a few e-mails around the world and we receive all the details of what's on anywhere, anytime. Or we can download the latest movie by crunching in our credit card numbers. We've got portable phones, texting, and fax on board. Nowadays all we have to do is make a call and use our GPS (Global Positioning System) to give us an exact location and in 20 minutes the delivery pizzas arrive. It's great sleeping out under the stars. We love it when darkness falls. Did I mention we've got quartz halogen floodlights mounted to the front and back and one million-candle power searchlights on the roof? There's a mosquito killer, intruder alarm, and with the air conditioning on full blast, there's always a nice cool breeze. The kids adore being camped out by the lakeside under the moonlight watching TV with some popcorn freshly made in the microwave. Dad spends hours in the shower while Mom heats TV dinners in the Dutch oven (at least I think Mom said that microwave came from Holland).

We've got everything a person needs to survive in the wilderness: the latest technology in walking boots, electrically heated battery-operated socks for chilly days, ear muffs that turn into sleeping bags, snow shoes, snow chains, winches, shovels, shortwave CB radio, moose repellent, night-vision binoculars, digital duck calls, electronic firelighters, you name it. We're 100 percent self-sufficient camperoos.

What's that? You ask me why we're parked here on the side of the freeway? Well, the truth of it is…everything's closed and we forgot to get gas!

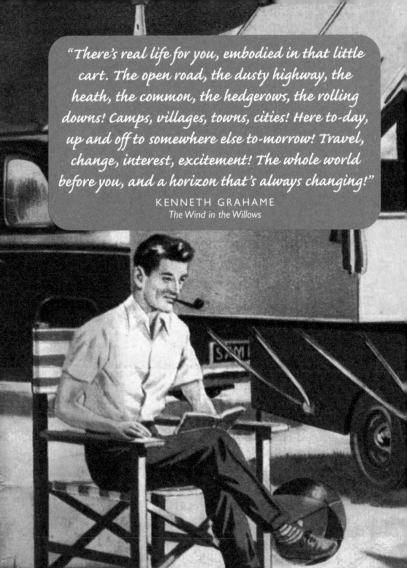

"There's real life for you, embodied in that little cart. The open road, the dusty highway, the heath, the common, the hedgerows, the rolling downs! Camps, villages, towns, cities! Here to-day, up and off to somewhere else to-morrow! Travel, change, interest, excitement! The whole world before you, and a horizon that's always changing!"

KENNETH GRAHAME
The Wind in the Willows

The High School Boys in Summer Camp

by

H. IRVING HANCOCK

After the meal was over the boys sat around the camp for a few minutes. Each hated to be the first to make a move toward the drudgery of dish-washing and camp cleaning.

"After we get things to rights," inquired Reade, "what is to be the programme for the day?"

"There's a pond east of us that is said to hold perch," Dave answered. "I'm going to take fishing tackle and go in search of a mess of fish. Anyone going with me?"

"I will," offered Danny Grin.

"As for me," spoke up Tom, "I have a line on a place where blueberries grow in profusion. Harry, will you go along with me and pick berries?"

"If it isn't over five miles away," Hazelton assented cautiously.

"Then what are we going to do!" asked Greg Holmes, turning to Prescott.

"From the plans we've heard laid down," smiled Dick, "I think we will have to stay right here and keep the prowler from dropping in to carry away the rest of our provisions."

"Bother such sport as that!" snorted Greg.

"Humph! It may turn out to be the liveliest sport of all," declared Dick dryly. "Certainly if that fellow turns up it will take two of us to handle him with comfort. He's a tough customer."

"Dan, you always were an artist with a shovel," suggested Darry insinuatingly. "Suppose you get out the spade and see what sort of perch bait you can turn up in this neighbourhood."

"Me?" drawled Dalzell protestingly. "Shucks! I'm no good at finding bait. Never was."

"Get the spade and try," ordered Darry. "If you don't find some bait we'll have to put off fishing until some other day."

That brought Dan to terms. He shouldered a spade, picked up an empty vegetable can and started away, while Dave began to sort tackle and to rig on hooks suitable for catching perch. Tom and Harry started in to unpack supplies from a pair of six-quart pails that they needed for the morning's work.

"Say, hear that, fellows!" demanded Tom, straightening up suddenly. From the distance to the northward came a dull rumbling sound.

"Thunder?" suggested Danny Grin, glancing wonderingly up at the clear sky.

"If there's a storm coming it will upset a day's berrying," Reade announced. ☞

"Fellows," Dick broke in, "it's a rumbling, yet it doesn't sound just like thunder, either. It sounds more like—"

"Cavalry on a gallop," suggested Greg.

"Just what it does sound a lot like," Prescott nodded. Then he dropped to the ground, holding one ear close to the earth.

"And, whatever the rumble may be," Prescott went on, "it travels along the ground. Just get your ears down, fellows."

"It's something big, and it's moving this way," cried Dave.

"It can't be cavalry," Tom argued. "There are no manoeuvres on; there is no state camp ever held in this part of the state, either. What do you—"

But Dick Prescott was up on his feet by this time. Furthermore, he was running. He stopped at the base of the trunk of the first tall tree. Up he went with much of the speed of a squirrel. Higher and higher he made his way among the branches.

"Say, be careful there, Dick!" called Tom Reade, warningly. "If you get a tumble—"

"I'm not a booby, I hope," Dick called down, as he went to still loftier heights. He was now among the slender uppermost branches…Even Dick Prescott might readily enough snap a branch now, and come tumbling to earth.

"Stop!" warned Tom. "If you don't you'll butt your head into a cloud, the first thing you know."

"Can you see anything?" called Danny Grin.

"I see quite a cloud of dust to the northward."

"How far off?" asked Dave.

"About a mile, I should say, and it's headed this way, coming closer every minute."

"What's behind the cloud? Can you make out?" Greg bawled up.

"I'm trying to see," Dick replied. "There, I got a glimpse then. It's some kind of animals, heading for this camp at a gallop."

"It can't be cavalry," shouted Reade. "You don't see any men, do you?"

"No," Prescott called down, shielding his eyes with one hand. "Say, fellows!"

"Have you guessed what it is?" demanded Harry Hazelton.

"I know what it is—now!" Dick answered. Then he began to descend the tree with great speed.

"Careful, there!" shouted Tom Reade. "That isn't a low baluster you're sliding down."

"Keep quiet, until I reach the ground," gasped Dick. As he came nearer those below saw that he looked truly startled....

"We've got to get out of here, fellows!" he called. "You know the trick that cattle-owners have in this part of the county of turning their cattle out to graze in one bunch. That bunch is headed this way—hundreds strong, and it's going to rush through this camp, trampling everything in the way!"

Star Gazing

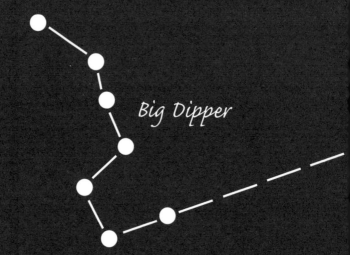

Big Dipper

As you sit back on a starlit night beholding the wonders of the universe remember that what you are seeing is exactly as it was seen by generation after generation.

Those stars that we witness from the surface of this spinning globe are there each night. Four minutes earlier over the horizon each night they appear, two hours over the span of a month. If you check a star's position tonight at a particular time and then check it again tomorrow at the exact same time, you will make an interesting discovery. The star will have moved one degree of arc countclockwise if you are in the

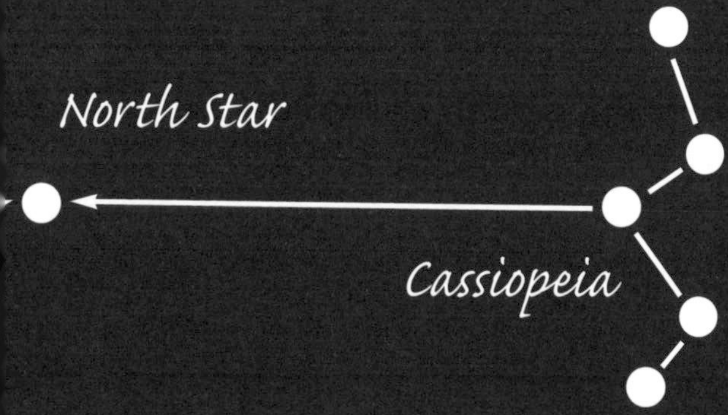

North Star

Cassiopeia

Northern Hemisphere or one degree of arc clockwise if you happen to be in the Southern Hemisphere.

Whether you are positioned in the Northern or Southern Hemisphere determines which constellation you can use to determine your north or south direction to get your bearings.

If you are looking at the Northern Sky, the main constellations to learn are the Ursa Major, also known as the Big Dipper or the Plow, and Cassiopeia. We can use them to locate Polaris, also known as the polestar or the North Star. The North Star forms part of the Little Dipper handle, ☞

which can sometimes be confused with the Big Dipper. So to prevent this, use both the Big Dipper and Cassiopeia together to position the North Star as they are always directly opposite each other, rotating counterclockwise around Polaris, which remains constant in the center. Locate the Big Dipper, which is the bright seven-star constellation, shaped like a dipper. If you look at the two stars that form the extreme outer lip, you will be looking at the "pointer stars," so-called because if you were to draw a line to join them and continue it outward about five times that length it will bring you to Polaris, the North Star.

Double check this by locating Cassiopeia with its five stars that form a "W" shape lying on its side. Draw a straight line between the center of the "W" to where the handle of the Big Dipper joins the dipper, and the North Star should be positioned exactly halfway along that line. Draw a mental line from the North Star to the Earth, and you have the direction of the North Pole and your bearings.

In the Southern Hemisphere the Southern Cross is an ideal signpost to the south. It is made up of five stars, the brightest four of which form a cross that is tilted to its side. Look at the two stars that make the long axis. These are the pointer stars. Imagine them joined by a line and that line continuing exactly five times as long as the distance between

Southern Cross

Imaginary Point

Southern Landmark

the two pointers, then from the imaginary point where that line ends, draw another line directly down to Earth, and this is the general direction of the South Pole. Spot a landmark to give you the direction on land.

We are the Red Men

We are the Red Men, tall and quaint,
In our feathers and war paint:
Pow-wow, pow-wow,

CHORUS
We're the men of the Old Dun Cow.
All of us are Red Men,
Feathers-in-our-head-men,
Down-among-the-dead-men,
Pow-wow, pow-wow.

We can fight with sticks and stones,
Bows and arrows, slings and bones,
Pow-wow, pow-wow,
CHORUS

We come back from hunts and wars,
Greeted by our long-nosed squaws,
Pow-wow, pow-wow,
CHORUS

We like Girl Guides, yes we do
Eat their innards in a stew
Pow-wow, pow-wow!
CHORUS

EXTRACT FROM

The Camp Fire Girls at Long Lake

by

JANE L. STEWART

"I suppose we could get some more wood and throw it on the fire. It would be warm enough then, if we got a couple of blankets to wrap around us."

"I think it's a good idea to stay awake and keep watch, anyhow, in case he should come back. Then, if he saw someone sitting up by the fire he would be scared off, I should think."

"All right. Slip in as quietly as you can, Dolly, and get our blankets from the tent, while I put on some more wood. There's lots of it, that's a good thing. There's no reason why we shouldn't use it."

So, while Dolly crept into their tent to get the blankets, Bessie piled wood high on the embers of the camp fire, until the sparks began to fly, and the wood began to burn with a high, clear flame. And when Dolly returned she had with her a box of marshmallows.

"Now we'll have a treat," she said. "I forgot all about these. I didn't remember I'd brought them with me. Give me a pointed stick and I'll toast you one."

Bessie looked on curiously. The joys of toasted marshmallows were new to her, but when she tasted her first one she was prepared to agree with Dolly that they were just the things to eat in such a spot.

"I never liked them much before," said Bessie. "They're ever so much better when they're toasted this way."

"They're good for you, too," said Dolly, her mouth full of the soft confection. "At least, that's what everyone says, and I know they've never hurt me. Sometimes I eat so much candy that I don't feel well afterward, but it's never been that way with toasted marshmallows. My, but I'm glad I found that box!"

Campfire Science

A campfire is not only the heart of camp, it can also mean the difference between survival and death, depending on your circumstances. A fire is primarily useful for cooking food, but perhaps rather surprisingly, it makes the food you cook go even further by providing warmth, which in turn means that one is burning fewer calories trying to produce body heat. There is the psychological comfort factor of having light in a dark place and the physical comfort provided by its warmth and tranquilizing meditative quality of its sounds, smells, and appearance. Not only will it help to deter wild animals from your camp during the dark hours, but it will also help to keep the nastier airborne insects at bay while your wet pants and socks are drying beside it. The important thing to keep in mind is that fire is a triangle. The three sides represent air, heat, and fuel.

Remove any of these and the fire will go out. Provide the correct ventilation and fuel, and your fire will burn steadily—too much ventilation will swiftly devour your fuel supply; too little ventilation will produce more smoke than flame and eventually smother it. If you avoid a fierce fire, it will need less fuel, less servicing, and the glowing embers will serve you well. Your campfire will warm you, protect you, boil your water, and cook and preserve your food. It will give you and those around you somewhere magical to gather after dark to sing songs, tell tales, and generally enjoy sharing in the camaraderie of camping.

PRIMUS AT THE NORTH

PRIMUS AT THE SOUTH

TRADE MARK
PRI-MUS

North - Sout
PRIMU

Original Patentees & Manufacturers, A/B. B.

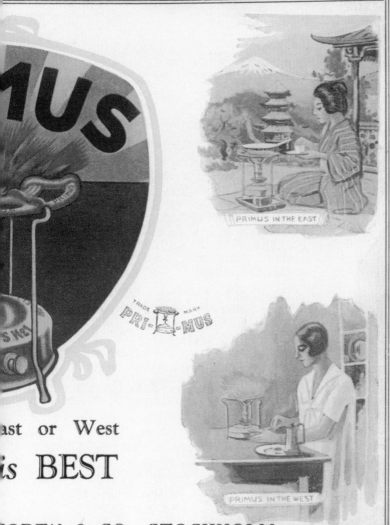

PRIMUS IN THE EAST

TRADE MARK
PRI-🔆-MUS

PRIMUS IN THE WEST

…ast or West

…is BEST

…ORTH & CO., STOCKHOLM, SWEDEN

Campfire Baked Apples

SERVES 2

> 2 apples
> 4 tbsp dried fruits
> 4 tbsp nuts
> 1½ tsp cinnamon sugar, made of ½ cup
>   sugar and 1 tsp cinnamon
> 1 tsp butter or margarine

1. Core the apples, leaving their bottoms intact. Stuff each cavity with fruits and nuts of your choice, packing the mixture fairly tight. Sprinkle with cinnamon sugar and dot with butter. Wrap the apple in a double thickness of aluminum foil, twisting the ends to form an easy handle for gripping from the top.

2. Place the apples right side up on the coals. Bake for 12 to 18 minutes, turning occasionally, or until the apples yield slightly when pushed with a gloved hand. Before serving, open the foil and let cool for a few minutes.

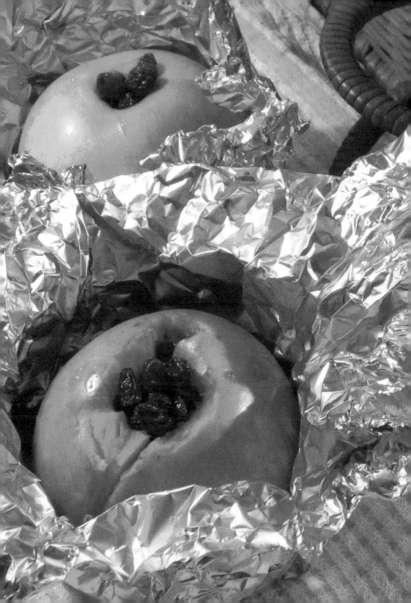

Huckleberry Finn

by

MARK TWAIN

I knowed I was all right now. Nobody else would come a-hunting after me. I got my traps out of the canoe and made me a nice camp in the thick woods. I made a kind of a tent out of my blankets to put my things under so the rain couldn't get at them. I catched a catfish and haggled him open with my saw, and towards sundown I started my camp fire and had supper. Then I set out a line to catch some fish for breakfast.

When it was dark I set by my campfire smoking, and feeling pretty well satisfied; but by and by it got sort of lonesome, and so I went and set on the bank and listened to the current swashing along, and counted the stars and drift logs and rafts that come down, and then went to bed; there ain't no better way to put in time when you are lonesome; you can't stay so, you soon get over it.

And so for three days and nights. No difference—just the same thing. But the next day I went exploring around down through the island. I was boss of it; it all belonged to me, so to say, and I wanted to know all about it; but mainly I wanted to put in the time. I found plenty strawberries, ripe and prime; and green summer grapes, and green razberries; and the green blackberries was just beginning to show. They would all come handy by and by, I judged.

Find a Good Campsite

Choosing a good campsite doesn't only mean searching for a great view and pleasant ambience, it can also mean the difference between surviving and not surviving under certain conditions. It's probably best to take everything into consideration when setting up camp—avoid rushing into things just because you think you'll get a great view of the stars or the lake from a certain position.

Stop and look around you. What does the site tell you? Are you on a hilltop and therefore exposed to wind? Then move down on the leeside and seek another spot. Are you standing in a deep hollow or at the bottom of a valley? This site is likely to be damp, has the potential to flood, and is most liable to night frost. Search for another base camp immediately.

Is the site you've found on a spur leading down to water? It may look appealing and attractive, but watch out for tracks because this is probably a route that animals take to reach their watering place.

There are so many factors to consider when choosing a campsite. Are you under branches that could come down in a storm? Is there any sign that bees, wasps, or hornets are nesting nearby? Is the ground hard and uneven? Are there anthills around you? Is the tree you're planning on camping beside liable to be struck by lightning? If you notice any of the above, find another campsite. ☞

The proximity to water and firewood should play a part in your decision, as these are the two most important things to see you through your camping experience. However, it's advisable not to camp too close to water as it could rise in a rainstorm. Still, calm waters and warm nights can provoke insects. Remember to look for high watermarks and stay out of old, dry watercourses, which could flash flood from rainfalls miles away in the hills.

Your shelter is one of the most important components when it comes to the camping experience. Your tent provides shade from the hot sun, repels the wind, and keeps you dry when it rains. A shelter will keep you warm when the temperatures plummet at night, and it provides you with a safe, secure, and comfortable place to get a night's rest.

Be sure to remove any sharp stones from underneath where your tent is being pitched. Make sure you are aware of what is immediately around you, then clear the areas for the tent and the campfire before darkness falls or the weather breaks. It's important to make this the priority on your list, as you don't want to be caught out without a shelter, desperately searching for equipment in the dark.

The key to enjoyable camping is all about preparation—choosing a suitable campsite is your first step to a sucessful and fun camping vacation.

Taps

(SING WITH REVERENCE.)

Day is done
Gone the sun
From the lakes
From the hills
From the sky
All is well
Safely rest
God is nigh.

Fading light
Dims the sight,
And a star gems the sky,
Gleaming bright,
From afar,
Drawing nigh,
Falls the night.

Thanks and praise,
For our days,
Neath the sun,
Neath the stars,
Neath the sky,
As we go,
This we know,
God is nigh.

The famous bugle call known as "Taps," which is played at lights out or bedding-down time was composed back during the Civil War. While encamped at Harrison's Landing, Brigadier General Daniel Butterfield, commander of the Third brigade of the first division of the Army of the Potomac's fifth corps, observed that his brigade's bugle call caused confusion in camp, because it could not be distinguished from that of other brigades. So he devised a unique bugle call for them. Then, after noting that the regulation evening bugle call was neither musical nor soothing, he composed an alternative tune for his bugler, that became "Taps." Soon the entire Army of the Potomac was using the tune at lights out, and today it remains the official army regulation bugle call.

By sight and scent of morning smoke,
By evening camp-fire's mirth,
By deep-sea call and foaming green,
By new stars' gleam and glow …

JAMES HEBBLETHWAITE
"Wanderers"

Campfire Entertainment

Entertaining others around the campfire is one of the most traditional and enjoyable ways to interact when camping. It will also take your mind off all those other tedious camp duties, such as gathering firewood, doing the dishes, collecting water, etc. Think up activities and games that will involve everyone. It's a sociable way to continue to enjoy the warmth of the campfire, way into the night.

SHAMAN

Each player takes a turn to enter the campfire circle and reenact an episode from the day or previous days—with no speaking whatsoever. The player who guesses correctly goes next.

CHARADES

Like Shamen, Charades is another great game to play around a campfire. A player takes the center and, without speaking, uses a predescribed gesture to describe a book, a play, a movie, an opera, or musical. Player's should indicate how many words are in the title. Long words can be ☞

☞ further broken down into syllables using a gesture. For example, tapping three fingers on their arm can mean there are three syllables. They should indicate which word in the title has the three syllables again by holding up the right number of fingers. Each word of the title is acted out in no fixed order until the players guess correctly what that word is and eventually decipher what the title of the book, movie, or chosen topic actually was. The person who guesses correctly gets to go next.

MURDER

This is a great game if there are five or more people around the campfire. Get every seated person to close their eyes. An individual is elected to walk behind the circle of people two or three times. And while doing so, without anyone else knowing, they touch one of the sitters. That chosen person is the Assassin!

Once chosen everybody can open their eyes again and no one but the person who chose them and the Assassin themselves know who's who. The Assassin must try to kill off the circle one by one by blinking at them without being noticed or caught by the others, who can challenge at any time if they think they know who it is. If they are wrong, they lose their life. This continues until there is either a capture or a wipeout.

Morning in Camp

BY HERBERT BASHFORD

A bed of ashes and a half-burned brand
Now mark the spot where last night's campfire sprung
And licked the dark with slender, scarlet tongue;
The sea draws back from shores of yellow sand,
Nor speaks lest he awake the sleeping land.
Tall trees grow out of shadows; high among
Their sombre boughs one clear, sweet song is sung,

In deep ravine by drooping cedars spanned,
All drowned in gloom; a flying pheasant's whirr
Rends morning's solemn hush; gray rabbits run
Across the clovered glade, while far away
Upon the hills each huge, expectant fir
Holds open arms in welcome to the sun—
Great, pulsing heart of bold, advancing day!

Forest Fires

One of the most destructive forces known is when fire gets out of control and becomes wildfire. In 90 percent of these incidences, the cause comes down to human negligence, while only a few are caused by natural occurrences, such as lightning strikes. Wherever there is dry undergrowth, shrub, bush, forest, or grassland, there is the potential for a wildfire, and where there are such catastrophic fires, there are men and women risking their lives to try to bring them back under control.

Conditions are perfect for a forest fire if the weather has been dry and hot, there is a dry wind blowing through, or the sky shows signs of a thunderstorm. It's important that every camper takes the time to prevent wildfires by using their common sense and making a commitment to care about their actions when camping.

If you smoke outdoors, don't do it in anyplace where it is prohibited. Stay away from any combustible materials and be sure to always extinguish and dispose of any smoking materials after use. Never ever flick lit cigarette or cigar butts into vegetation.

If you must drive into the wilderness, don't park your vehicle on dry grass. SUVs should be equipped with spark arresters. Never ignore the regulations about burning off rubbish and cuttings. When camping, be careful where you store combustible materials and never ever use stoves, fueled lanterns, and heaters inside of a tent. After a campfire has been burning, always make certain that everything is out and not smoldering. Always return your site to the way it was when you found it.

If you should ever be involved in a wildfire, leave the area immediately by established trails, roads, and routes, and contact a Ranger right away. If routes are blocked, then head for the nearest lake, river, or stream.

Old Smokey the Bear has been urging us for well over half a century to help prevent forest fires so take heed.

Always check that it's OK to have a campfire in your desired location before you settle down for the night. And finally, always remember Smokey's original catchphrase, dating back to 1944: "Only you can prevent forest fires." Smokey's catchphrase has recently been updated in response to wildfire outbreaks:

"Only you can prevent wildfires."

SMOKEY THE BEAR

Worse than speeding, mister. You threw a lighted cigarette out of the car and started a forest fire!

Baden-Powell and Boy Scouts

It's strange to think that the scouting movement came about as a direct result of war, but it did. Its foundations can be traced to the Seige of Mafeking in South Africa during the Boer War (1899–1902). A certain commanding officer named Lord Robert Baden-Powell was charged with defending the town from the attacking Boers who outnumbered his own troops by eight to one. With odds stacked highly against them, Baden-Powell took it upon himself to form the Mafeking Cadet Corps entirely of boy volunteers with the goal of them supporting his troops in defending the town, which they did superbly. Each Cadet received a special Corps insignia badge of a compass point and a spearhead. Their founder, Baden-Powell, returned a national hero, and wrote a training manual entitled "Aids to Scouting" (in 1899), which became a best-seller and a fundamental resource for teachers and youth organizations.

At the turn of the century Baden-Powell was introduced to the work of American author Ernest Thompson Seton who had written another influential manual "The Birchbark Roll of the Woodcraft Indians." The two men combined their ideas on youth-training programs, and in 1907 Baden-Powell had rewritten much of his own earlier book for a younger readership. Baden-Powell was also conducting a key experiment by gathering 22 boys from mixed social ☞

backgrounds to camp for a week on Brownsea Island near Poole Harbour in Dorset and there he pioneered his methods, which were published in installments in a boys' magazine. These articles were destined to become a book titled *Scouting For Boys*, which was undoubtedly the very first version to exist of the *Boy Scout Handbook*.

Then things began to generate a momentum of their own. Up and down the country, boys were beginning to form their own Scout Patrols, and they turned to Baden-Powell for leadership. Soon there were to be Sea Scouts, Air Scouts, and Wolf Cubs. The spear and compass point motif of the Mafeking Cadets was changed to the now internationally familiar Fleur-de-lys motif, and scouting spread worldwide.

Today, it is probably the biggest youth organization in the world uniting boys and girls through a global philosophy to help young people develop physically, mentally, and spiritually through a nonformalized educational process that places its emphasis on practical outdoor and community-spirited activities and self-sufficiency. It's a long way from those humble and heroic beginnings, and scouts may no longer resemble little soldiers from the Boer War in their pioneer hats and short trousers, but at the heart of it all is the guiding light of the founding father Sir Robert Baden-Powell and his belief in preparing the youth of the world for a better life.

Thus the Birch Canoe was builded
In the valley, by the river,
In the bosom of the forest;
And the forest's life was in it,
All its mystery and its magic,
All the lightness of the birch-tree,
All the toughness of the cedar,
All the larch's supple sinews;
And it floated on the river
Like a yellow leaf in Autumn,
Like a yellow water-lily.

HENRY WADSWORTH LONGFELLOW
"The Song of Hiawatha"

How to Build a Bark Canoe

by

PETER KALM

About two o'clock this afternoon we arrived at Fort Anne. We stayed here all this day, and the next, in order to make a new boat of bark, because there was no possibility of going down the river without it.

The making of our boat took up half yesterday, and all this day. To make such a boat, they pick out a thick tall elm, with a smooth bark, and with as few branches as possible. This tree is cut down, and great care is taken to prevent the bark from being hurt by falling against other trees, or against the ground. For this reason, some people do not cut down the trees, but climb to the top of them, split the bark, and strip it off, which was the method our carpenter took. The bark is split on one side, in a straight line along the tree, as long as the boat is intended to be; at the same time, the bark is carefully cut off a little way on both sides of the slit, that it may more easily separate.

The bark is then peeled off very carefully, and particular care is taken not to make any holes in it; this is easy when the sap is in the trees, and at other seasons the tree is heated by the fire, for that purpose. The bark thus stripped off is spread on the ground, in a smooth place, turning the inside downwards, and the rough outside upwards; and to stretch it better, some logs of wood or stones are carefully put on it, which press it down. Then the sides of the bark are gently bent upwards, in order to form the sides of the boat; some sticks are then fixed into the ground, at the distance of three or four feet from each other, in the curved line, which the sides of the boat are intended to make, supporting the bark intended for the sides. The sides of the bark are then bent in the form, which the boat is to have, and according to that form the sticks are either put nearer or further off.

The ribs of the boat are made of thick branches of hickory, which are tough and pliable. They are cut into several flat pieces, about an inch thick, and bent into the form, which the ribs require, according to their places in the broader or narrower part of the boat. When thus bent, they are put across the boat, upon the back, or its bottom, pretty close, about ten inches from each other.

The upper edge on each side of the boat is made of two thin poles, of the length of the boat, which are put close together, on the side of the boat, and are flat, where they are to be joined. The edge of the bark is put between these two poles, and sewed up with threads, mouse-wood bark, or other tough bark, or with roots.

But before it is thus sewed up, the ends of the ribs are likewise put between the two poles on each side, taking care to keep them at some distance from each ☞

other. After that is done, the poles are sewed together, and when bent properly, both their ends join at each end of the boat, where they are tied together with ropes. To prevent the widening of the boat at the top, three or four bands are put across it, from one edge to the other, at the distance of thirty or forty inches from each other.

These bands are commonly made of hickory, on account of its toughness and flexibility, and have a good length. The ends are put through the bark on both sides, just below the poles, which make the edges; they are bent up above those poles and twisted round the middle part of the bands, where they are carefully tied by ropes. As the bark at the two ends of the boat cannot be put so close together as to keep the water out, the crevices are stopped up with the crushed or pounded bark of the red elm. Some pieces of bark are put upon the ribs in the boat, without which the foot would easily wear through the thin and weak bark below, which forms the bottom of the boat.

For better security some thin boards are commonly laid at the bottom, which may be trod upon with more safety. The side of the bark, which has been upon the wood, thus becomes the outside of the boat, because it is smooth and slippery, and cuts the water more easily than the other. The building of these boats is not always quick; for sometimes it happens that after peeling the bark off an elm, and carefully examining it, it is found pierced with holes and splits, or it is too thin to venture one's life in.

In such a case another elm must be looked for; and it sometimes happens that several elms must be stripped of their bark, before one is found fit for a boat. That which we made was big enough to bear four persons, with our baggage, which weighed somewhat more than a man.

All possible care must be taken in rowing on the rivers and lakes of these parts with a boat of bark. For as the rivers, and even the lakes, contain numbers of broken trees, which are commonly hidden under the water, the boat may easily run against a sharp branch. This would tear half the boat away, if you rowed on very fast. The people in it would be in great danger, where the water is very deep, especially if such a branch held the boat.

To get into such a dangerous boat must be done with great care, and for the greater safety, without shoes. For with the shoes on, and still more with a sudden leap into the boat, the heels may easily pierce through the bottom of the boat. This might sometimes be attended with very disagreeable circumstances, especially when the boat is near a rock, and close to a sudden depth of water; and such places are common in the lakes and rivers here.

Zum Gali Gali

"Zum Gali Gali" is a world famous Guiding song that marks the participation of Jewish youth in the world of scouting. It comes from a song sung by the *chalutzim* (pioneers) or settlers of the modern land of Israel and it passed on to new generations via synagogue youth groups in the 1950s. It literally means "The pioneer (*chalutz*) is meant for work (*avodah*); work (*avodah*) is meant for the pioneer (*chalutz*)."

There is some speculation as to whether the words "Zum Gali" are derived from the Hebrew for Galilee, "Ha Galil," and that the chant means "To Galilee."

Wherever its roots lie, it's a song that is often sung by people in Israel while they are working, offering the hope that: "Ha shalom le maan ha amin (Peace shall be for all the world), Ha amin le maan ha shalom (All the world shall be for peace)."

Zum, gali-gali-gali,
Zum gali-gali,
Zum, gali-gali-gali,
Zum gali-gali.

(One group continues to sing this behind the verses.)

Eh-chalutz leh mon avo-dah,
Avo-dah lah mon eh-chalutz.

Eh-chalutz leh mon avo-dah,
Avo-dah lah mon eh-chalutz.

From the dawn till setting sun
Every one finds work to be done.
From the dawn till night does come
There's a task for everyone.

Eh-chalutz leh mon avo-dah,
Avo-dah lah mon eh-chalutz.
Eh-chalutz leh mon avo-dah,
Avo-dah lah mon eh-chalutz.

From the dawn till setting sun
Every one finds work to be done.
From the dawn till night does come
There's a task for everyone.

Zum, gali-gali-gali,
Zum gali-gali,
Zum, gali-gali-gali,
Zum gali-gali.

Zum,

Zum.

EXTRACT FROM

The Camp Fire Girls at Long Lake

by

JANE L. STEWART

There were cold chicken, and rolls, and plenty of fresh butter, and new milk, and hardboiled eggs, that the girls had stuffed, and a luscious blueberry pie that Bessie herself had been allowed to bake in the big farm kitchen. They made a great dinner of it, and Walter was loud in his praises.

"That certainly beats what we have out here most days!" he said. "We have plenty—but it's just bread and cold meat and water, as a rule, and no dessert. It's better than they get at most farms, though, at that."

When the meal was finished the girls quickly made neat parcels of the dishes that were to be taken back, and all the litter that remained under the tree was gathered up into a neat heap and burned.

"My, but you're neat!" exclaimed Walter, as he watched them.

"It's one of our Camp Fire rules," explained Margery. "We're used to camping out and eating in the open air, you know, and it isn't fair to leave a place so that the next people who camp out there have to do a lot of work to clean up after you before they can begin having a good time themselves. We wouldn't like it if we had to do it after others, so we try always to leave things just as we'd like to find them ourselves. And it wouldn't be good for the Camp Fire Girls if people thought we were careless and untidy."

Camping in the Woods. A Good Time Coming, after a painting by A. F. Tait

The Tepee

What we have come to know as the tepee is actually from the Sioux word "Tipi," which means "for living in." To the Native American Plains Indians, the tepee was considered home. It was an extremely practical structure providing warmth in winter months and a cool shelter during summer. Tepee are robust, extremely portable, and easy to erect.

The tall, sleek conical shape followed a circular base, which may have come about through the Indians belief in the circular nature of the world and life itself.

Complete with its striking elongated smoke flaps the tepee served permanent and temporary housing needs, while also providing shelter for hunting camps. A well-constructed tepee could be expected to last for many years. It is thought that it was the buffalo hunters of the Great Plains who were responsible for its design. It is excellent for withstanding high winds, while the flaps outside, which are adjusted with the use of poles, allowed for better ventilation and dispersal of smoke from the internal fires that would be burning inside them.

A tepee is composed of its cover, the poles, and a tepee liner that all work together. The poles—which are harvested from the tall, slender, and appropriately named lodge-pole pines that grow in dense forests—form the framework to support the cover and on which to hang the liner. A correctly pitched tepee has its cover staked a few inches above the ground while the interior liner hanging from the inside edge of the poles serves not only to seal the bottom of the tepee but also to create an effective chimney to draw the smoke from the open fire out through the adjustable smoke flaps.

While other forms of tented structures were (and sometimes still are) difficult to pitch, poorly ventilated, and badly suited to the seasons, the tepee was highly efficient. Its simple yet effective design showed that Native Americans were not only highly practical people, but also very artistic—they often painted designs on the animal hide covers with "paints" made from the juice of berries and other plants. They believed that these designs protected against misfortune and sickness.

Between 12–17ft/3.5–5m in diameter, a tepee provided the ideal environment. Ultimately, it acted as a shelter. However, within them Native Americans could live close-knit family lives, and offer congenial hospitality to a large group of guests in a perfect meeting place. Erected correctly, the cone would be positioned, tilted slightly to run with the wind, becoming steeper at the back, with the smoke flaps positioned on the more gently sloping front edge at apposition above the fire, which would have been positioned closer to the door. This served a number of purposes, including better ventilation, the wherewithal to withstand driving winds, and to increase headroom inside.

Twisted Willow Campfire Bread

SERVES 4

12oz/1½ cups/350g flour
pinch of salt
14 tsp baking soda
1oz/2 tbsp/25g butter, diced small

1. Trim 4 willow (or other suitable) branches into long sticks for cooking the bread over a fire or barbecue. Scrub them well and then soak them in water for at least half an hour so they won't char.
2. Sift the four, salt, and baking soda into a bowl. Add the butter and cut in until the flour mixture resembles crumbs. Mix in just enough cold water to make a stiff dough, then set aside to rest for a few minutes.
3. Cut the rested dough into 4 pieces and then twist each piece around the top of a prepared willow stick. Cook over the fire or barbecue, turning from time to time to ensure even cooking, until golden brown all over.

Indian Flat Breads

SERVES 6

14oz/1¾ cups/400g flour
2 tbsp baking powder
large pinch of salt
2 tbsp powdered milk
1¼ cups/300ml warm water
vegetable oil, for frying

1. Sift the flour, baking powder, salt, and powdered milk into a large mixing bowl. Add about three-quarters of the warm water and mix in well. Continue adding the warm water a little at a time just until the mixture forms a soft dough that is not sticky. Cover and let rest for about 30 minutes.
2. Divide the dough into 6 portions, roll into balls, and then flatten these into rounds about ¼in/5mm thick.
3. Heat about ¼in oil in a frying pan until quite hot and then cook the rounds one at a time until golden brown on both sides. Drain briefly on crumpled paper towels. Serve while still nice and hot.

The Sacred Pipe

The Native Indian peace pipe is often portrayed in films being used by tribal elders. Sitting cross-legged around campfires in tepee, they pass the pipe between themselves and white men who come to offer peace treaties. But the Sacred Pipe or Calumet is much deeper in meaning and importance than that. It is steeped in legend and significance and is as vital to the indigenous people's beliefs as anything any Christian or believer of other doctrine might hold sacred.

The pipe was given to the Native American peoples by different sources according to their own legends. But one that is widespread is that the Great White Buffalo Calf Maiden came to the Indians and showed them how to use it, explaining that the smoke issuing from the mouth is the path for purest truth that rises to the Great Spirit. It provides the Great Spirit with a bridge between the heavens and Mother Earth. What is burned in the pipe's bowl represents every part of creation, and those who share in the smoking of the sacred pipe make clear their true good intentions to the Great Spirit, Creator of all things.

One person leads the ceremony. He holds the bowl of the pipe in his left hand, the stem in his right. When they are pieced together the pipe becomes sacred. He points the bowl and stem to the east, the south, the west, and the north. He touches it to the ground and points it to the heavens thanking

the Great Spirit, Mother Earth, Father Sky, the seasons, and the spirit guides. Pinches of tobacco and sweet-smelling herbs, barks of red willow, wild cherry, white willow, birch, and roots of bayberry, bearberry, mugwort, lovage, and others that have been harvested and deemed significant by the village's society of sacred tobacco blenders are added along the way. The pipe is then smoked and passed from one person to the next around the sacred circle as prayers are made for knowledge, peace, and guidance.

Be Prepared

If there are six little words to set the cash registers ringing they must be, "What camping equipment do I need?" Sales personnel are standing waiting for you to arrive. There is no polite word to describe what a lot of the equipment out there amounts to in terms of usefulness. It represents a waste of money, a waste of space, and with the added weight, a waste of energy. It's like asking the proverbial question, "How long is a piece of string?" Before investing any money in camping equipment, first invest a little time in what you want to do and find out about what you need in order to do it through the library, on the Internet, or via your local Boy Scouts or Campfire Girls. But never rush in.

Ask yourself some vital questions. Where are you going and for how long? Is food available there, and more importantly, drinking water, or will you have to carry it with you? Consider the climate and the terrain and what would constitute being the appropriate clothing. Are there any other considerations, perhaps medical ones?

If you have miles to hike then proper hiking boots are essential. Being far away from anywhere in bad terrain with only a pair of broken or ill-fitting boots would be a nightmare. If you are carrying everything in on foot you'll need a good-sized, manageable backpack that the weather won't penetrate. Make certain it's fully adjustable, with a comfortable hip belt.

If you're near water, then seal everything in strong plastic bags inside your rucksack. This will help to keep all of your equipment dry should the worst happen.

Don't skimp on a cheap tent with hundreds of heavy poles, lines, and pegs everywhere. Invest a little more and get one that is waterproof with a groundsheet sewn in and zipped flaps. A dome tent is excellent because you can sit upright inside them very comfortably, and many have little ante-chambers in which to store kit, supplies, and wet clothing; they even offer some privacy. Many come with lightweight flexible rods and can be pitched in a matter of moments with a few stakes to keep them from flying away. Tents with an inner and outer layer are excellent insulators from the cold but also keep things cool in the heat. They're extremely waterproof and are available in a variety of sizes, shapes, and weights. The best advice is to visit a reputable supplier armed with as much knowledge as you can absorb, listen to the information, and try out everything before buying it. No one should ever buy a tent without first trying it out for size.

Similarly with sleeping bags, there are many types, shapes, sizes, and weights. You need a good idea of the temperature extremes. If it's too light, you're likely to get cold during the night—too heavy and it will become a burden. ☞

☞ Try to avoid buying gadgets. They may sound useful but most aren't and just take up room and add weight. Be sure to carry matches in a watertight container, some candles, a flint with a steel saw-striker, a compass, a good multipurpose knife, a flexible saw, a magnifying glass, a needle and thread, and tweezers. Each camper should have a mess tin for cooking, eating, and drinking, fish hooks and line, a selection of adhesive bandages, and other medical supplies (see list on pages 232–241). A small solid-fuel cooking stove and a kettle for boiling water will always come in handy. Have a set of dry clothes sealed in plastic bags. You'll come to appreciate this change of clothes if it's raining the next hiking day.

Dried food takes up little room and adds little weight but is greatly appreciated out there in the dark and cold. Take some stock cubes, packets of hot chocolate, dried soup mixes, and instant mashed potatoes. Dried fruits, such as apricots and pears make great snacks or cooked desserts. Always keep salt and a small mix of spices with you, which will make even the most basic meals taste exotic. A small flashlight is useful provided you remember to switch it off when you aren't using it! Take extra batteries along if you've got the space.

Whatever your budget, being prepared is an achievable goal and a must for a fulfilling and rewarding camping experience that you will always remember.

The Camp

BY MARY ROBINSON

Tents, marquees, and baggage-waggons;
Suttling-houses, beer in flagons;
Drums and trumpets, singing, firing;
Girls seducing, beaux admiring;
Country lasses gay and smiling,
City lads their hearts beguiling;
Dusty roads, and horses frisky,
Many an Eton Boy in whisky;
Tax'd carts full of farmers' daughters;
Brutes condemn'd, and man who slaughters!
Public-houses, booths, and castles,
Belles of fashion, serving vassals;
Lordly gen'rals fiercely staring,
Weary soldiers, sighing, swearing!
Petit-maitres always dressing,
In the glass themselves caressing;
Perfum'd, painted, patch'd, and blooming
Ladies—manly airs assuming!
Dowagers of fifty, simp'ring,
Misses for their lovers whimp'ring;
Husbands drilled to household tameness;
Dames heart sick of wedded sameness.
Princes setting girls a-madding,

Wives for ever fond of gadding;
Princesses with lovely faces,
Beauteous children of the Graces!
Britain's pride and virtue's treasure,
Fair and gracious beyond measure!
Aid-de-camps and youthful pages,
Prudes and vestals of all ages!
Old coquets and matrons surly,
Sounds of distant hurly-burly!
Mingled voices, uncouth singing,
Carts full laden, forage bringing;
Sociables and horses weary,
Houses warm, and dresses airy;
Loads of fatten'd poultry; pleasure
Serv'd (to nobles) without measure;
Doxies, who the waggons follow;
Beer, for thirsty hinds to swallow;
Washerwomen, fruit-girls cheerful,
Ancient ladies—chaste and fearful!
Tradesmen, leaving shops, and seeming
More of war than profit dreaming;
Martial sounds and braying asses,
Noise, that ev'ry noise surpasses!
All confusion, din, and riot,
Nothing clean—and nothing quiet.

Oak logs will warm you well,
That are old and dry;
Logs of pine will sweetly smell,
But the sparks will fly.

AUTHOR UNKNOWN
"The Woodcutter's Song"

Pork 'n' Beans

8oz/225g salt pork or fatty bacon, diced
1 onion, chopped
2 garlic cloves, finely chopped
1½ lb/675g cooked beans, such as
    navy or kidney beans, or two 14-oz/
    400-g cans of beans, drained and
    rinsed
4–6 tbsp tomato ketchup
salt and pepper
4oz/125g cheddar cheese, grated
    (optional)

1. Fry the pork or bacon, stirring regularly, until the fat runs.
Add the onion and garlic, and sauté until the onion is
translucent. Remove the contents from the skillet, leaving as
much of the fat as possible.
2. Add the beans to the skillet and lightly mash them with a
fork as you mix them with the hot fat.
3. Add the bacon and onion mixture to the skillet and mix
with the beans, ketchup, and salt and pepper to taste. Add a
little water if the mixture isn't creamy enough.
4. Cover, set over a very gentle heat, and cook about 1 hour,
until a crust forms on the bottom of the skillet.
5. Sprinkle with the cheese to serve (optional).

How to Start a Fire

There are many ways and methods of starting a fire. Some are more simple than others to achieve and most of the techniques take a little time and patience to master.

METHOD ONE (*useful in a survival situation*)
- **Use the spark from a car or strong torch battery**
- **Bring together the ends of two pieces of wire running from the positive and negative terminals of the battery**
- **The spark jumps just before the wires touch together**
- **Catch the spark in your tinder or a piece of gasoline-dampened rag**

METHOD TWO (*as used by cowboys and even today's soldiers*)
- **Remove the bullet end from a round of ammunition**
- **Pour out half of the propellant from the cartridge**
- **Stuff a small piece of rag into the cartridge**
- **Load cartridge into the weapon**
- **Fire weapon into the ground discharging the now smoldering rag**
- **Smoldering rag is left lying on tinder and remaining propellant from the cartridge** ☞

👉 METHOD THREE

- **Lenses and magnifying glasses, even broken soda bottles can be used to start a fire (broken glass and bottles regularly cause accidental fires when discarded by careless campers)**
- **Prepare your tinder**
- **Hold lens in path between the sun and the tinder, adjusting until the glass catches the sunlight**
- **Keep a steady hand until tinder and undergrowth begins to catch light**

However, the methods that bring about the most pleasure and the greatest peace of mind are those that can be used in almost any situation. These are the natural methods that require a bit of human ingenuity, some patience, trust in one's own ability, and a lot of friction.

FIRE BOW METHOD

This technique uses the friction of a hardwood spindle rotated on a softwood base to produce fine wood dust tinder, and then heat.

- **Ensure that both the hardwood spindle and the softwood base are dry**
- **The spindle should be even and straight**
- **Gouge a small indentation at the rear end of the baseboard**
- **Cut a cavity below the indentation in which to place your tinder**
- **Using a strong hazel or bamboo-type shoot create your bow using a hide lace, strong twine, or a bootlace**
- **Locate a palm-sized stone with a depression in it or something similar**
- **Wind the bowstring once around the spindle, loop facing outward not toward the bow**
- **While kneeling on one knee use your other foot to hold down the baseboard**
- **Place bottom end of spindle into the indentation on the baseboard**
- **Place the stone on the top end of the spindle and bear down on it with pressure from one hand** ☞

☞ while the other hand draws the bow back and forth, spinning the spindle against the baseboard where it will try and drill through until the glowing tip drops like a glowing cigarette end onto the tinder in the cavity beneath
- **Nurse the glowing ember to life with some gentle blowing until tinder ignites**
- **Place ignited tinder at the base of your campfire**

If you achieve this, you will have succeeded in joining the select brotherhood of mankind who carry with them the secret of how to make fire, something that links each generation back to the very first time fire was made in this manner. A box of matches will never have the same meaning to you again.

FIRE PLOUGH METHOD
- **Locate a dry softwood baseboard**
- **Cut a groove running along its length**
- **Plough a hardwood shaft back and forth along the length of the groove continuously, while applying downward pressure**
- **The ploughing action will first produce tinder and then a glowing tip with which to ignite your fire**

THE HAND DRILL METHOD

- **Make a softwood baseboard**
- **Find a dry, hollow softwood stem to make a spindle, preferably with a pith core**
- **Carve a "V"-shape notch at its end to take tinder**
- **Cut a small indentation to take the shaft just beside the tip of the "V"**
- **Place the bottom of the spindle into the indentation on the baseboard**
- **Continuously roll the spindle between the palms of the hands, running your hands down its length as you do so to increase the friction**
- **When the tip glows, blow gently to ignite tinder**

Flint against steel will also produce good sparks. Many camping suppliers sell flints with a small steel-saw blade attached, which is really helpful when starting fire.

Anna Karenina

by

LEO TOLSTOY

Vronsky was staying in a roomy, clean, Finnish hut, divided into two by a partition. Petritsky lived with him in camp too. Petritsky was asleep when Vronsky and Yashvin came into the hut. "Get up, don't go on sleeping," said Yashvin, going behind the partition and giving Petritsky, who was lying with ruffled hair and with his nose in the pillow, a prod on the shoulder. Petritsky jumped up suddenly onto his knees and looked round. "Your brother's been here," he said to Vronsky. "He waked me up, damn him, and said he'd look in again." And pulling up the rug he flung himself back on the pillow. "Oh, do shut up, Yashvin!" he said, getting furious with Yashvin, who was pulling the rug off him. "Shut up!" He turned over and opened his eyes. "You'd better tell me what to drink; such a nasty taste in my mouth, that..."

"Brandy's better than anything," boomed Yashvin. "Tereshtchenko! Brandy for your master and cucumbers," he shouted, obviously taking pleasure in the sound of his own voice.

"Brandy, do you think? Eh?" queried Petritsky,

blinking and rubbing his eyes. "And you'll drink something? All right then, we'll have a drink together! Vronsky, have a drink?" said Petritsky, getting up and wrapping the tiger-skin rug round him. He went to the door of the partition wall, raised his hands, and hummed in French, "There was a king in Thule."

"Vronsky, will you have a drink?"

"Go along," said Vronsky, putting on the coat his valet handed to him.

"Where are you off to?" asked Yashvin. "Oh, here are your three horses," he added, seeing the carriage drive up. "To the stables, and I've got to see Bryansky, too, about the horses," said Vronsky.

Vronsky had as a fact promised to call at Bryansky's, some eight miles from Peterhof, and to bring him some money owing for some horses; and he hoped to have time to get that in too. But his comrades were at once aware that he was not only going there. Petritsky, still humming, winked and made a pout with his lips, as though he would say: "Oh, yes, we know your Bryansky."

"Mind you're not late!" was Yashvin's only comment; and to change the conversation: "How's my roan? Is he doing all right?" he inquired, looking out of the window at the middle one of the three horses, which he had sold Vronsky.

"Stop!" cried Petritsky to Vronsky as he was just going out. "Your brother left a letter and a note for ☞

☞ you. Wait a bit; where are they?"

Vronsky stopped.

"Well, where are they?"

"Where are they? That's just the question!" said Petritsky solemnly, moving his forefinger upwards from his nose.

"Come, tell me; this is silly!" said Vronsky smiling.

"I have not lighted the fire. Here somewhere about."

"Come, enough fooling! Where is the letter?"

"No, I've forgotten really. Or was it a dream? Wait a bit, wait a bit! But what's the use of getting in a rage. If you'd drunk four bottles yesterday as I did you'd forget where you were lying. Wait a bit, I'll remember!"

Petritsky went behind the partition and lay down on his bed. "Wait a bit! This was how I was lying, and this was how he was standing. Yes, yes, yes! Here it is!"— and Petritsky pulled a letter out from under the mattress, where he had hidden it. Vronsky took the letter and his brother's note. It was the letter he was expecting—from his mother, reproaching him for not having been to see her—and the note was from his brother to say that he must have a little talk with him. Vronsky knew that it was all about the same thing. "What business is it of theirs!" thought Vronsky, and crumpling up the letters he thrust them between the buttons of his coat so as to read them carefully on the road. In the porch of the hut he was met by two officers; one of his regiment and one of another.

Vronsky's quarters were always a meeting place for all the officers.

"Where are you off to?"

"I must go to Peterhof."

"Has the mare come from Tsarskoe?"

"Yes, but I've not seen her yet."

"They say Mahotin's Gladiator's lame."

"Nonsense! But however are you going to race in this mud?" said the other.

"Here are my saviors!" cried Petritsky, seeing them come in. Before him stood the orderly with a tray of brandy and salted cucumbers. "Here's Yashvin ordering me a drink a pick-me-up."

"Well, you did give it to us yesterday," said one of those who had come in; "you didn't let us get a wink of sleep all night."

"Oh, didn't we make a pretty finish!" said Petritsky. "Volkov climbed onto the roof and began telling us how sad he was. I said: 'Let's have music, the funeral march!' He fairly dropped asleep on the roof over the funeral march."

"Drink it up; you positively must drink the brandy, and then seltzer water and a lot of lemon," said Yashvin, standing over Petritsky like a mother making a child take medicine, "and then a little champagne—just a small bottle."

"Come, there's some sense in that. Stop a bit, Vronsky. We'll all have a drink."

Backyard Camping

Any child can benefit from the camping experience, even if their first trip is only as far away as their own backyard. It's an excellent stepping-stone to the real wilderness adventure for adults just as much as their children. It gives new campers the chance to make mistakes and to learn from them, to experiment with what is and isn't necessary, and to discover those things that are vital to take and those that just weigh you down. It's a character-building exercise and a wonderful family bonding experience too.

Most important, you will learn whether or not the tent you chose, or that the salesman convinced you to buy, was the right choice or not. In fact, why not see if you can rent a tent that is like the one you have your eye on and give it a test drive in your backyard camp? It could save you a great deal of time and money and make the difference between whether your camping expedition is enjoyable or a disaster. There are a great many camping equipment outlets so do some research.

Depending on local restrictions, the backyard is an excellent place to learn the secrets of making a campfire and to experiment with camp craft. Remember to return the land to its previous state after the campfire has burned out. With some backyard drill, pitching a tent can be achieved in a couple of minutes which, in a real-life camping situation can make a world of difference, especially if it is pouring with rain. Striking and packing away camp equipment successfully takes practice. If backpacking, tents need to be carefully packed away, sleeping bags properly rolled and stowed, and knapsacks packed with care. Practicing in the backyard is far from a waste of time.

What the experience will inform you about is the stockpile of things you didn't or wouldn't have needed, and shows up the shortfall of items that would have been useful or preferable. It's better to be able to run from the backyard into your own kitchen for a utensil than be stuck at an inland lake miles from anywhere without the things you need.

Try out campfire recipes, perfect your campfire cooking skills (it's a whole different world), and get to know the tricks of successful cooking using a Dutch oven. Work out sleeping arrangements, and determine the warmth and comfort factor of your sleeping bags. See how well you can entertain yourselves and each other, and discover how effective your waterproofing is. The important thing is not to cheat.

While it is perfectly OK to run indoors and substitute utensils and grab things you find to be vital, it is not OK to run inside and watch your favorite TV program, or to grab more candy, make telephone calls, etc. And what if the weather breaks? Well, this is a period of discovery, it could just as easily break when you are away in the wild, so why not ride it out and see how it goes? If it all becomes just too much you can always make a run for the backdoor.

If you go down to the woods today,

You're sure of a big surprise.

CHILDREN'S SONG "The Teddy Bears' Picnic"

The Truce of the Bear

BY RUDYARD KIPLING

Yearly, with tent and rifle, our careless white men go
By the Pass called Muttianee, to shoot in the vale below.
Yearly by Muttianee he follows our white men in—
Matun, the old blind beggar, bandaged from brow to chin.

Eyeless, noseless, and lipless—toothless, broken of speech,
Seeking a dole at the doorway he mumbles his tale to each;
Over and over the story, ending as he began:
"Make ye no truce with Adam-zad—the Bear that walks like a Man!

"There was a flint in my musket—pricked and primed was the pan,
When I went hunting Adam-zad—the Bear that stands like a Man.
I looked my last on the timber, I looked my last on the snow,
When I went hunting Adam-zad fifty summers ago!

"I knew his times and his seasons, as he knew mine, that fed
By night in the ripened maizefield and robbed my house of bread.
I knew his strength and cunning, as he knew mine, that crept
At dawn to the crowded goat-pens and plundered while I slept.

"Up from his stony playground—down from his well-digged lair—

Out on the naked ridges ran Adam-zad the Bear—

Groaning, grunting, and roaring, heavy with stolen meals,

Two long marches to northward, and I was at his heels!

"Two long marches to northward, at the fall of the second night,

I came on mine enemy Adam-zad all panting from his flight.

There was a charge in the musket—pricked and primed
     was the pan—

My finger crooked on the trigger—when he reared up like
     a man.

☞ "Horrible, hairy, human, with paws like hands in prayer,
Making his supplication rose Adam-zad the Bear!
I looked at the swaying shoulders, at the paunch's swag and swing,
And my heart was touched with pity for the monstrous,
     pleading thing.

"Touched with pity and wonder, I did not fire then…
I have looked no more on women—I have walked no more with men.
Nearer he tottered and nearer, with paws like hands that pray—
From brow to jaw that steel-shod paw, it ripped my face away!

"Sudden, silent, and savage, searing as flame the blow—
Faceless I fell before his feet, fifty summers ago.
I heard him grunt and chuckle—I heard him pass to his den.
He left me blind to the darkened years and the little mercy of men.

"Now ye go down in the morning with guns of the newer style,
That load (I have felt) in the middle and range (I have heard) a mile?
Luck to the white man's rifle, that shoots so fast and true,
But—pay, and I lift my bandage and show what the Bear can do!"

(Flesh like slag in the furnace, knobbed and withered and grey—
Matun, the old blind beggar, he gives good worth for his pay.)
"Rouse him at noon in the bushes, follow and press him hard—
Not for his ragings and roarings flinch ye from Adam-zad.

"But (pay, and I put back the bandage) this is the time to fear,
When he stands up like a tired man, tottering near and near;
When he stands up as pleading, in wavering, man-brute guise,
When he veils the hate and cunning of his little, swinish eyes;

"When he shows as seeking quarter, with paws like hands in prayer
That is the time of peril—the time of the Truce of the Bear!"

Eyeless, noseless, and lipless, asking a dole at the door,
Matun, the old blind beggar, he tells it o'er and o'er;
Fumbling and feeling the rifles, warming his hands at the flame,
Hearing our careless white men talk of the morrow's game;

Over and over the story, ending as he began—
"There is no truce with Adam-zad, the Bear that looks like a Man!"

Make a Simple Tepee

To make a simple tepee, you will need
four poles. Choose the desired height
for your tepee and make sure that the
four poles are of equal length. Bind the
poles together near the top with a
string, but not all the way. (See fig. 1)

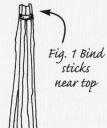

Fig. 1 Bind
sticks
near top

Fig. 2
Triangular
shape

This way they can swing out at
the bottom to make a cone
shape. (See fig. 2)

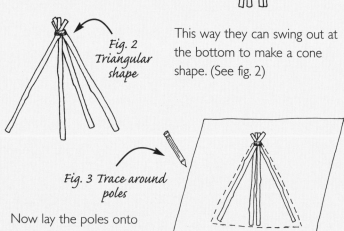

Fig. 3 Trace around
poles

Now lay the poles onto
some sheets of newspaper
taped together. Spread out two of the poles on the paper
to make the shape of one of the sides of your tepee. Trace
around the poles and you should have drawn a triangle.
(See fig. 3)

Fig. 4 Cut out template

Cut out the paper triangle, lay it onto a large dustsheet, and trace the triangle shape onto the sheet. (See fig. 4)

Now lift the paper and lay it with its long side against the long side you've just drawn and again trace around it onto the dustsheet. Do this twice more until you have four triangles drawn on the sheet. Cut all the way around the outside edge of the entire polygon. (See fig. 5)

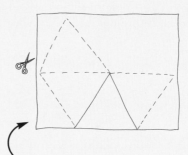

Fig. 5 Cut around polygon shape

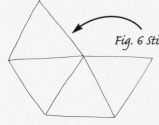

Fig. 6 Stitch long ends together

Next stitch the two long ends together. (See fig. 6) 👉

Fig. 7 Cut off tip

🖎 Cut off the tip of the fabric the same length as the part of the poles that are above the binding. The ends of the poles will go through this hole. Now if you slide the poles inside the structure and splay them in the upright position you will have a four-sided tepee. (See fig. 7)

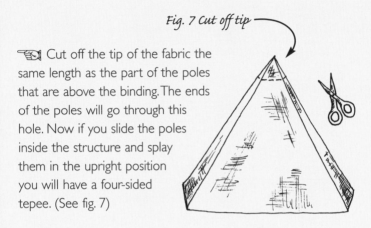

All that is needed is to cut a semicircular hole at the bottom of one of the sides. (See fig. 8). Decorate the tepee with some Indian motifs.

Fig. 8 Slide poles in

Smoke Signals

Mankind has had to develop ways to communicate important messages over long distances. After all, we haven't always had the telephone, cellular phone, and global-satellite-positioning systems. And being industrious and highly intelligent creatures, we came up with all manner of means to do this. We put out rock formations where they could be seen from the hilltops above, or cut into the landscape to create silhouettes on the horizon, used fire or flashing sunlight on reflective surfaces, and even used our own body to send signals.

As we became more elaborate and bound by technology, Samuel Morse invented the Morse code, a series of short and long beeps or pulses sent from a transmitter to a receiver. For example, ...---... is the international distress signal of the Morse code letters—SOS, which stands for Save our Souls.

Smoke signals are also a very effective method of sending a message over a great distance. However, they are also open to the sight of other people, so friends and enemies would both be likely to see the same message as it was being sent. For this very reason there is no standardized code, as such, for smoke signals. The secrets they transmitted would be devised and understood privately using a predesignated code.

Smoke signals were originally used by the Plains Indians as beacons and a method of sending messages over long distances. They could communicate efficiently with them over vast distances, signaling the location of water, the route of the enemy, or the time of a council meeting.

To make your own smoke signals: First light a clear, hot fire. Cover it with green vegetation or rotten wood so that it sends up a solid column of dense smoke. By spreading and lifting a blanket over this smoldering mound, the column of smoke can be cut up into long or short pieces. For example, one steady column of smoke would indicate, "Here is camp," to someone who is lost. Today smoke signals still provide an excellent way of attracting the attention of searching aircraft or passing ships from the shoreline if you are stranded.

Ask any Boy Scout, military person, woodsman, camper, or cowboy, and they will tell you that, universally, three signals of any kind, whether sent by gunshots, whistles, shouts, waves, or smoke signals, indicate danger and are intended as a call for help. No one should ever ignore three signals or send them as a joke.

If using smoke signals to communicate with friends, remember to decide first what your code is going to be. Then ensure that both parties are positioned on high, adjacent hills or mountains at a visible point where the fires will be made. Make your fire and use your blanket, tarp, or other covering to control the release of smoke into the air in a series of puffs.

Great Spirit, Creator of us all,
Creator of all things, Creator
of the four directions, Mother
Earth, and Father Sky, we
offer this pipe to you.

NATIVE AMERICAN PIPE CEREMONY

Indian Blankets

It is a little difficult perhaps, for those of us used to modern comforts to reflect on a time when one of the most important items known to mankind was a blanket. But without the blanket, particularly the Indian blanket or the trading blanket, the history of the colonization of the Americas would have been altogether different.

The blanket had played a key role in the lives of Native Americans well before white explorers began setting foot on their land. The Indians used blankets woven from plant fibers and animal fur, eventually weaving them from cotton and wool by hand. They would trade them between themselves for other things, so they always had a value. Maybe that was because the blanket featured in everything that occurred in Indian life, from the cradle to the grave. Blankets were the gifts given in celebration of weddings and the births of new children. They were offered as tokens of gratitude and often used to clear debts. A person's status could be calculated by their personal holdings of blankets. Blankets could be worn when it was cold, or provide shade when the sun was too hot. They could even provide life-saving shelter and made a fine burial shroud.

There are records of the Native Americans trading with newly arrived European traders dating back to the early 1600s. Usually the Native Americans traded beaver pelts for European blankets. They preferred white, red, and blue blankets most of all. A white blanket could be traded for anything up to six beaver pelts, which made them very valuable to possess. They only really became known as "Indian blankets" because of their designs. However, the majority of Indian Trading Blankets were factory-made by Pendleton, a company that is still renowned to this day for producing high-quality blankets. Curiously, it was only recently that someone actually thought of commissioning a Native American to design blankets.

As we sit in the relative comfort of today and look back, it's hard to understand the importance that came to be heaped upon these simple items. Yet, as he was surrendering in the final years of the 1890s, Chief Joseph of the Nez Perce is reported to have made the following statement:

"It is cold and we don't have any blankets. The little children are freezing to death. My people, some of them, have run away up into the hills and have no blankets, no food. No one knows where they are, perhaps they are freezing to death. Give me time to look for my children and see how many of them I can find. Maybe I shall find them among the dead. Hear me, my chiefs. I am tired; my heart is sick and sad. From where the sun now stands, I will fight no more forever."

Who would have imagined that so much celebration, ordinary life, ritual, survival, comfort, turmoil, and grief could be woven together into such a simple thing as a blanket.

Campfire Side-Skills

Every camper needs to learn and practice a few craft skills and survival techniques. From whittling a simple wooden spoon to finding your way without a compass, there's a Boy Scout bursting to get out of all of us.

FIND YOUR WAY

Did you know that it's possible to find the direction of north and south by simply using a wristwatch with an hour and minute hand? It's an easy technique that has saved the lives of many downed pilots, lost soldiers, and stranded motorists, in all manner of scenarios.

If you are in the Northern Hemisphere, hold your watch horizontal on the flat of your hand. Point the hour hand at the sun then cut the distance in half between the hour hand and the twelve mark, and this will give you the north-south line. For example, if the sun is at four o'clock, the hour hand points to the sun and the point midway between it and the twelve will be two so north will be in the direction of the two mark, with south in the direction of the eight mark. (Be sure your watch is set to true local time.)

In the Southern Hemisphere, the same method can be used, but it's slightly different. Here you should hold your watch horizontally flat on the palm of your hand and point the twelve at the sun. The point halfway between the twelve and the hour hand will give you the north-south line. For example, when the twelve is pointing in the direction of the sun and it is eight o'clock, then north will point in the direction of ten and south will be in the direction of the five mark. Practice and check your findings with your compass or known directions toward certain landmarks.

MAKE A WOODEN SPOON

Use the tip of your sharp knife to carve a spoon shape onto a flat piece of wood, always moving the blade away from your body. Gradually whittle away the waste wood until you achieve the desired shape. Don't rush or you are likely to make mistakes and you'll have to start again. ☞

☞ MAKE A CAMP SEAT

Nothing is more uncomfortable than sitting on a hard and damp ground when you are trying to enjoy the warmth of an evening's campfire. Of course, you could always use a simple dry log to sit on. However, you can impress your fellow campers by making a functional camp seat or small bench. Make two simple, low "A" frames and lash each frame a few inches from the top with string or binding. Rest a sturdy bough between the two frames and take a seat! It's always useful to have a portable seat that can be moved easily around the campsite.

REACH NEW HEIGHTS WITH A TAPERED LADDER

Sometimes it's necessary to access items that have been stored up high or to reach tree branches that are beyond our grasp. It's wise to store your food away from your campsite in a food safe, hanging from a tree branch in order to keep away scavenging animals. To build a useful ladder, find a pair of long, strong wooden poles and some sturdy shorter pieces to form the crosspieces or rungs. Bind these crosspieces tightly across the longer poles, which should be set at an angle of about 1ft/30cm at the top to 2–2½ft/60–76cm at the bottom. The lashed rungs will not slip down the longer wooden poles as readily when you climb them.

HANG UP A FOOD SAFE

To prevent ground-dwelling creatures and insects from ruining your food, find a shaded area, and tie a rope from a sturdy branch. Get a sealable tin box, and tie it to the branch.

Birdcalls

Camping is the ideal
excuse to get to
know more about
wildlife, particularly
birds. From the
comfort of your tent or from
a secluded spot in the
wilderness it is easy to tune
your ears into the sounds that are being
bantered back and forth. With a little bit of practice, you can
soon reach a stage where it is possible to identify the birds
that are in the proximity purely by their songs and calls. It is an
extremely rewarding pastime and is great fun played as a
group or family game.

A good way to build up a knowledge of which bird is
saying what is to adopt a mnemonic system of
remembering each call. These are little
sound phrases that are associated with
each species so that when you hear
the actual call in nature you can easily
identify the bird making the noise.
Some examples might include
the American Black
Oystercatcher who produces a

rapid clipped "wheep, wheep, wheep…" call, or the American Coot with its loud and clear "kuh-uk! khu-uk!", or the Black-Capped Chickadee who goes through life calling out for "Phoebe."

When using mnemonics to characterize the vocalizations of birds you'll soon realize that there is far more going on out there unseen than you could ever have imagined. Some bird sounds are far too complex to characterize adequately or accurately in this way. And there are so many birdcalls in the world it would be impossible to memorize every single one. An excellent way of building up a stockpile is to visit the Internet, which is filled with different mnemonic lists. Print some off for the areas where you intend to camp, such as European birds, Eastern American birds, Mexican birds, and so forth. Often online enthusiasts place small sound samples of the actual calls on their websites. These enable you to compare the listed mnemonics with what you actually hear while camping. ☞

The best time to listen out for birdcalls is in the morning—during the hour before sunrise. The chorus of birdsong is beautiful to hear, and it's a real test of your knowledge to pick out individual voices in the choir and identify them.

Serious bird watchers will often build up a comprehensive "lifelist" of birds they have seen and note down corresponding birdcalls as a record. It's a great way to keep track of your observations and helps to organize the calls that you have heard in a coherent way. Identifying birds and birdcalls is a popular and challenging pastime for many and lifelists provide a means by which fellow enthusiasts can share their discoveries with one another. Fanatic birdwatchers seeking to discover new species to add to their lists are called "twitchers." The word supposedly refers to the uncontrollable twitches of excitement that a birdwatcher experiences when coming across a bird for

the first time.
There is even a Code
of Birding Ethics collated by
the American Birding Association
(ABA) that sets out guidelines and
principles for enjoying and respecting
birds and wildlife, the environment, and the
rights of other birdwatchers.

Nothing compares to the pleasure of authenticating a type
of bird by spotting it through binoculars and identifying it by
its appearance. A good pair of binoculars is a wonderful
investment. They needn't be expensive or big and cumbersome.
With advances in lens-making technology, new coatings, and
better light response, a pair of binoculars that easily slips into
the pocket will do the job perfectly well. Do a little research
and try some out to discover what works best for you.

Choose a good pocket-sized field guide for your specific
destination to help you when bird-watching. The best will
have an easy format of indexing so you can look up the bird
you've spotted quickly. Some even have a mnemonic clue to
describe the call, which will help you confirm your sighting.
Soon, everywhere you go, you will be identifying bird songs
and calls, recognizing some as old friends, and hearing others
for the first time.

Indoor Camping for Kids

Here is something to entertain young children on a rainy day when everybody is forced to remain indoors.

Create an "outdoor-indoor" camping safari complete with tent, wildlife, and campfire.

Put together a rainy-day box for just such an occasion in which you should store:

- **An old double bedsheet**
- **A flashlight**
- **A printed Indian-style blanket**
- **A few clothespins**
- **A piece of cord or rope**
- **Six medium-sized rocks to act as weights**
- **Several dozen clean pebbles**
- **A sheet of red cellophane**
- **A small pile of sticks**
- **A sound-effect tape or CD of rainforest or woodland sounds**

In a room that has a clear floor space stretch the rope between two sturdy tying off places, about 3ft/1m high. Drape the double bedsheet lengthwise along the rope. Peg out the sides of the tent with the six medium rocks and you will have a makeshift tent! ☞

Now form a circle about 1½ft/46cm in diameter using small pebbles. Place the flashlight in the middle of the pebbles and lay the red cellophane over the top of it.

Using the pebbles as a support, make a tepee-shaped campfire, balancing the tips of the sticks against each other above the flashlight. (Make sure there's room to reach through the sticks to switch the flashlight on.)

Place the wildlife effects on the sound system and you have everything that's needed for a day of intensive imaginative play. It is amazing how quickly young minds can soak up the ambience.

As it grows darker (either close the curtains or dim the lights) tell the children that it's time to light the campfire. Switch on the flashlight which, shining through the red cellophane, will look like a glowing campfire.

Seat everyone around the campfire and tell ghost stories, sing songs, and play games. You could even pass around a bag of marshmallows. (Although toasting them over your flashlight campfire is probably out of the question!)

The Land of Story-books

ROBERT LOUIS STEVENSON

At evening when the lamp is lit,
Around the fire my parents sit;
They sit at home and talk and sing,
And do not play at anything.

Now, with my little gun, I crawl
All in the dark along the wall,
And follow round the forest track
Away behind the sofa back.

There, in the night, where none can spy,
All in my hunter's camp I lie,
And play at books that I have read
Till it is time to go to bed.

These are the hills, these are the woods,
These are my starry solitudes;
And there the river by whose brink
The roaring lions come to drink.

I see the others far away
As if in firelit camp they lay,
And I, like to an Indian scout,
Around their party prowled about.

So, when my nurse comes in for me,
Home I return across the sea,
And go to bed with backward looks
At my dear land of Story-books.

Davy Crockett

Davy Crockett was born in Tennessee in 1786, and in his lifetime became famous as a frontiersman with a reputation as an Indian fighter and bear killer. He is also associated with having a tendency to tell tall stories. He fought in the Creek War and was elected to the Tennessee State Legislature and eventually into congress. However, he found this boring, so in search of adventure, he took off to Texas where he was killed at the Alamo with several other legendary figures.

But of all the things this intrepid explorer and legend of a man became known for, the most famous was perhaps his hat, with its raccoon face at the front and hooped tail hanging down the back. That hat was to become a huge craze following the screening of the television series about him in the 1950s. It is said that because Disney brought the tale to TV before everyone had television sets in their family homes, viewing was something of a shared event. An entire gaggle of neighborhood children would watch the show together under one roof, leading to enthusiastic re-enactments of the Crockett programs in backyards and streets all over the United States. And every youngster simply had to have their very own Davy Crockett raccoon hat!

Sometimes there is confusion between Davy Crockett's hat and that of Daniel Boone (see page 260). But what Boone wore was a beaver hat. And although nobody can be certain, after the Battle of the Alamo, one of the women surviving the slaughter recalls recognizing Crockett's body by his peculiar cap, which must surely refer to his famous headgear.

EXTRACT FROM

David Crockett: His Life and Adventures

by

JOHN S. C. ABBOTT

They rode quietly along another hour and a half, when toward midnight they saw in the distance the gleam of camp-fires, and heard shouts of merriment and revelry. They knew that these must come from the camp of the friendly Cherokees, to which their Indian guide, Jack Thompson, was leading them. Soon a spectacle of wonderful picturesque beauty was opened to their view.

Upon the banks of a beautiful mountain stream there was a wide plateau, carpeted with the renowned blue-grass, as verdant and soft as could be found in any gentleman's park. There was no underbrush. The trees were two or three yards from each other, composing a luxuriant overhanging canopy of green leaves, more beautiful than art could possibly create. Beneath this charming grove, and illumined by the moonshine which, in golden tracery, pierced the foliage, there were six or eight Indian lodges scattered about.

An immense bonfire was crackling and blazing, throwing its rays far and wide through the forest.

Moving around, in various engagements and sports, were about forty men, women, and children, in the fringed, plumed, and brilliantly colored attire of which the Indians were so fond. Quite a number of them, with bows and arrows, were shooting at a mark, which was made perfectly distinct by the blaze of pitch-pine knots, a light which no flame of candle or gas could outvie. It was a scene of sublimity and beauty, of peace and loveliness, which no artist could adequately transfer to canvas.

"The best way to cook any part of a rangy ol' longhorn is to toss it in a pot with a horseshoe, and when the horseshoe is soft and tender, you can eat the beef."

AUTHOR UNKNOWN

Campfire Corn

SERVES 4

4 fresh cobs of corn
about 4 tbsp/2oz/50g butter
salt and pepper

1. Well ahead, pull out as much of the silk at the end of each cob as you can, but leave the corn in the husks. Soak the corn in cold water for at least an hour.
2. Drain the corn well and cook on the barbecue, turning from time to time, for about 30 minutes.
3. Remove the husks and serve with butter, and seasoning.

"Take the ears of Indian corn when in the Milk, and boil them almost enough to eat, then shell it, and spread it in a Cloth very thin, and dry it in the Sun till it shrinks to half its Bigness, and becomes very hard, then put it [in] any dry Cask, and it will keep the Year round. When you use it, you must put it in a Pot, and let it warm moderately over a Fire for three to four Hours, but which Means it swells considerably, then boil it till you find 'tis fit to eat."

BENJAMIN FRANKLIN'S RECIPE FOR DRYING CORN

The Wind in the Willows

by

KENNETH GRAHAME

"O, pooh! boating!" interrupted the Toad, in great disgust. "Silly boyish amusement. I've given that up long ago. Sheer waste of time, that's what it is. It makes me downright sorry to see you fellows, who ought to know better, spending all your energies in that aimless manner. No, I've discovered the real thing, the only genuine occupation for a lifetime. I propose to devote the remainder of mine to it, and can only regret the wasted years that lie behind me, squandered in trivialities. Come with me, dear Ratty, and your amiable friend also, if he will be so very good, just as far as the stable-yard, and you shall see what you shall see!"

He led the way to the stable-yard accordingly, the Rat following with a most mistrustful expression; and there, drawn out of the coach house into the open, they saw a gipsy caravan, shining with newness, painted a canary-yellow picked out with green, and red wheels.

"There you are!" cried the Toad, straddling

and expanding himself. "There's real life for you, embodied in that little cart. The open road, the dusty highway, the heath, the common, the hedgerows, the rolling downs! Camps, villages, towns, cities! Here to-day, up and off to somewhere else to-morrow! Travel, change, interest, excitement! The whole world before you, and a horizon that's always changing! And mind! this is the very finest cart of its sort that was ever built, without any exception. Come inside and look at the arrangements. Planned 'em all myself, I did!"

The Mole was tremendously interested and excited, and followed him eagerly up the steps and into the interior of the caravan. The Rat only snorted and thrust his hands deep into his pockets, remaining where he was.

It was indeed very compact and comfortable. Little sleeping bunks—a little table that folded up against the wall—a cooking-stove, lockers, bookshelves, a bird-cage with a bird in it; and pots, pans, jugs and kettles of every size and variety.

"All complete!" said the Toad triumphantly, pulling open a locker. "You see—biscuits, potted lobster, sardines—everything you can possibly ☞

want. Soda-water here—baccy there—letter paper, bacon, jam, cards, and dominoes—you'll find," he continued, as they descended the steps again, "you'll find that nothing what ever has been forgotten, when we make our start this afternoon."

"I beg your pardon," said the Rat slowly, as he chewed a straw, "but did I overhear you say something about 'we,' and 'start,' and 'this afternoon?'"

"Now, you dear good old Ratty," said Toad, imploringly, "don't begin talking in that stiff and sniffy sort of way, because you know you've got to come. I can't possibly manage without you, so please consider it settled, and don't argue—it's the one thing I can't stand. You surely don't mean to stick to your dull fusty old river all your life, and just live in a hole in a bank, and boat? I want to show you the world! I'm going to make an animal of you, my boy!"

"I don't care," said the Rat, doggedly. "I'm not coming, and that's flat. And I am going to stick to my old river, and live in a hole, and boat, as I've always done. And what's more, Mole's going to stick me and do as I do, aren't you, Mole?"

"Of course I am," said the Mole, loyally. "I'll always stick to you, Rat, and what you say is to be—has got to be. All the same, it sounds as ☞

if it might have been—well, rather fun, you know!" he added, wistfully. Poor Mole! The Life Adventurous was so new a thing to him, and so thrilling; and this fresh aspect of it was so tempting; and he had fallen in love at first sight with the canary-coloured cart and all its little fitments.

...Somehow, it soon seemed taken for granted by all three of them that the trip was a settled thing; and the Rat, though still unconvinced in his mind, allowed his good-nature to override his personal objections. He could not bear to disappoint his two friends, who were already deep in schemes and anticipations, planning out each day's separate occupation for several weeks ahead.

When they were quite ready, the now triumphant Toad led his companions to the paddock and set them to capture the old grey horse, who, without having been consulted, and to his own extreme annoyance, had been told off by Toad for the dustiest job in this dusty expedition. He frankly preferred the paddock, and took a deal of catching.

Meantime Toad packed the lockers still tighter with necessaries, and hung nosebags, nets of onions, bundles of hay, and baskets from the bottom of the cart. At last the horse was caught and harnessed, and they set off, all talking at once, each animal either trudging by the side of the cart or sitting on the shaft, as the humour took him. It was a golden afternoon. The smell of the dust they kicked up was rich and satisfying; out of thick orchards on either side the road, birds called and whistled to them cheerily; good-natured wayfarers, passing them, gave them "Good-day," or stopped to say nice things about their beautiful cart; and rabbits, sitting at their front doors in the hedgerows, held up their fore-paws, and said, "O my! O my! O my!"

Late in the evening, tired and happy and miles from home, they drew up on a remote common far from habitations, turned the horse loose to graze, and ate their simple supper sitting on the grass by the side of the cart. Toad talked big about all he was going to do in the days to come, while stars grew fuller and larger all around them, and a yellow moon, appearing suddenly and silently from nowhere in particular, came to keep them company and listen to their talk. At last they turned in to their little bunks in the cart; and Toad, kicking out his legs, sleepily said, "Well, good night, you fellows! This is the real life for a gentleman! Talk about your old river!"

"It is my desire to become a Camp Fire Girl and to obey the law of the Camp Fire, which is to Seek Beauty, Give Service, Pursue Knowledge, Be Trustworthy, Hold on to Health, Glorify Work, Be Happy. This law of the Camp Fire I will strive to follow."

JANE L. STEWART
The Camp Fire Girls in the Woods

Whole Red Snapper
with chili, herb, and lemon rub

SERVES 4

If you make the rub with fresh herbs, use it immediately.

4 large garlic cloves, finely chopped
finely grated peel of 2 lemons
2 hot red chilies, seeded and finely chopped
1 tsp chopped fresh rosemary,
    or ½ tsp dried rosemary
1 tbsp chopped fresh basil, or 1 tsp dried basil
2 tsp chopped fresh thyme leaves
    or ½ tsp dried thyme
1 tbsp brown sugar
2 whole red snapper, about 2½–3lb/1–1.5kg
    total weight, cleaned and scaled
salt and freshly ground black pepper

1. Fire up the barbecue to medium heat.

2. Mix together the garlic, lemon peel, chilies, rosemary, basil, thyme, and sugar, and season generously with salt and pepper.

3. Cut 3 or 4 slashes in each side of the fish, down to the bone. Rub with the herb mixture, making sure to get it into the slashes.

4. Place on barbecue grill or cook over campfire for 10–12 minutes, until golden and cooked through. Serve immediately.

We camp, and go, and care no jot
How soon, how far we roam ...
But each campfire has marked a spot
That men shall call their home.

ARTHUR W. JOSE
"The Pioneers"

Reading the River

Nobody in their right mind just jumps into a canoe on an unknown stretch of water, points it downstream, and heads off. There is a fine art to looking at a stretch of water and reading what is going on. Everything tells you something, from the changes in the characteristics of the water's surface, waves and eddies, to bends in the river, current direction, rocks, and shallows. People who understand these things have a feel for the river, the speed with which it flows, what lies upstream and downstream of them, and where the obstructions are likely to be. This is the only way to be really safe on the water. And once the doubt and fear have been removed, you are free to have fun.

It's no good taking off in a canoe, aiming it blindly downstream, and then discovering too late that around the first bend is a bridge with submerged pilings or a fallen tree waiting for you to ram into it. Is the speed of the water trying to warn you of the waterfall ahead or the rocky rapids coming up?

A skilled river reader will learn to identify the eddies along the way—these are the most important water features to know and understand. They are quiet areas of water which occur immediately downstream of an obstacle in a river and are easy to recognize as the current will become relatively calm. Eddies are good to aim for as they provide excellent rest stops to catch your next breath and observe the river ahead. A good tactic is to lay out a route that moves from eddy to eddy, section by section. The wise person pulls their boat up to a bank and then scouts ahead on foot, building up a picture of everything that is to come, the dangers to avoid, the excitement to enjoy—safely—and the energy to be rationed.

It is always better to work with the river than against it because that fight is a lost battle before it even starts. For those who like the quieter life, aim for the darker, still waters and avoid those places where any white water is showing. Use your ears for audible warnings of any major changes in the water flow nearby. Always be on the lookout for sudden major increases in the flow rate that may indicate rapids or falls ahead. Once you become experienced at reading the water, of recognizing obstacles, and are capable of evaluating the water flow, then it is likely that you will secure a good route, even in rapids. If the water is smooth with the surface rippling in a "V"-shape, and the sharp end of the "V"s are pointing downstream, then you will have found a clear chute to ride. However, if those ripples have the sharp end pointing upstream then chances are there's a rock there and that stretch is to be avoided.

Smooth humps in fast-flowing water are signs of submerged rocks. You'll soon begin to recognize dangerous hazards to avoid, but it won't come without a few hard knocks and good drenchings!

Summer Camps

Organized camping and summer camps are really more of an American institution than any other, although nowadays they are beginning to capture the global imagination. Today there are a wide range of seasonal camps geared at specific interests, from tennis coaching to outward bound pursuits, canoeing, climbing, and even camps for orchestral musicians and scientists.

These are all a long way from the earliest campfire gatherings, which stretch back to the moment humans first discovered the secret of creating fire. Every walk of life that involved traveling from one place to another involved camping. Armies were forever striking and breaking down their camps, and entire tribes and hunters camped where the hunting was. Drovers, cattlemen, Hussars, circuses, tramps, swagmen, pioneers, pilgrims, and the wet and weary all needed someplace safe to rest up before embarking on the next phase of their journeys through life. Their skills ☞

and traditions provided a great deal of the information and vital templates for what was later to become organized camping, passing on knowledge of everything from how to choose a campsite, to starting fires, trapping, and basic survival skills.

Sir Robert Baden-Powell is popularly imagined as the father of organized camping. However, he did not even publish *Scouting For Boys* until 1908 in England. It spread like wildfire to New Zealand and Canada within the same year. The Boy Scouts of America movement was born in 1910. But the story begins well before that, almost a full half century before.

The American summer camp was formed with the prime objective of creating a place where the youth of the day could come together to escape urban life. They lived together in a natural environment, which was structured to promote trust, remove any feelings of exclusion, and celebrate personal and group accomplishments. Summer camp is the place where children can prepare to be productive and healthy adults, through fun and games, trial and error, and adventure and discovery. Meanwhile their minds are awakened to the needs of others, and they are taught the importance of having a sense of community and protecting the natural world, while at the same time enjoying its pleasures.

It all began in the 1860s. School teachers Frederick and Abigail Gunn hiked their entire school to camp for two weeks at an outdoor destination. There the pupils enjoyed boating, fishing, and trapping. This is where today's breakaway curriculum concept camps were founded. Every step along the path has been an important discovery, incorporating the best traditions that have developed and remained over time.

Camps with various purposes have evolved over the years. For example, in 1876 Dr. Joseph Trimble Rothrock took "weakly boys out into camp life in the woods at his North Mountain School of Physical Culture…so that the pursuit of health could be combined with the practical knowledge outside usual academic lines." He was perhaps influenced by another project two years earlier. In 1874 the Young Women's Christian Association (YWCA) had put together a vacation project for unfortunate young women who had no other means of obtaining rest and recreation and were working themselves into early graves. Ten years later, the sibling YMCA took a few boys on a camping trip.

At the turn of the last century in 1900, a big leap forward was made when, in Salem, Massachusetts, The Boys Club ran a seven-week camp through the summer with more than 70 boys attending—a number that was to steadily grow each year into thousands of camps across America. In 1910 Alan Williams of the Sportsman's Show in New York founded the Camp Directors Association of America (CDAA). This provided a unifying standard for organized camps for young ☞

people. In 1924 it merged with The National Association of Directors of Girls' Camps, which was the foundation for what eventually became The American Camping Association (ACA).

Meanwhile more than 500 girls got together in 1914 for the first Camp Fire Girls camp ever. The Girl Scouts movement was founded in 1912 and within ten years had organized camps running throughout the US. By 1922, the worldwide scouting movement boasted more than a million members and by the outbreak of World War II it had grown in membership to more than three times that number.

Soon, camping magazines and publications became available. Camping was considered to be a very good thing to send your children off to do—and even to do yourself. National Parks began to make areas available for camping and set up recreational activities for organizations, and later for families and all comers. Standards were set for health and safety and for the types of program on offer. The goal of all providers was to gain the ACA camp accreditation, and an entire industry was in motion until the end of the 1960s. By that time almost 15 percent of the young people of America had had some form of organized camp experience.

Young people's literature was crammed with camp stories. All the exciting adventure movies involved camping. And television—as it became popular and accessible to the masses—made constant reference to summer camp and other organized camping. This whetted the appetites of young landlocked urbanites who longed for an experience in the wilderness with a canoe and a bow and arrow.

Wherever the camp and whatever the banner that flies above it, one thing, that universal symbol of comradeship, remains constant—the campfire. Tales are told, episodes from history are re-enacted, lessons are taught, great songs are sung, and lasting friendships are all forged around its glowing flames.

Camping Club

Although organized camping in America dates as far as the 1860s, recreational camping didn't really take root until the 1920s. The founder of modern recreational camping can be considered to be Thomas Hiram Holding, who wrote the first *Campers Handbook* in 1908. He caught the camping bug as a boy in 1853 crossing 1,200 miles of prairie in a wagon train among 300 people. In 1877 and 1878, he went on a canoeing-camping trip in the Scottish Highlands, and by 1901, he founded the first camping club in the world, the Association of Cycle Campers. By 1907, this merged with a number of other clubs to form the Camping Club of Great Britain and Ireland, and in 1909 the Camping Club was firmly established. Its first president was Captain Robert Falcon Scott, the famous Antarctic explorer.

With the advent of the affordable automobile, many Americans could escape the confines of their suburban neighborhood existence and explore their beautiful country, and thus another important camping club was born in 1919. This was centered around the Model T Ford and within eleven years, their ranks swelled to over 100,000 members, with Henry Ford and Thomas Edison as fellow campers.

Back in Britain and Europe, following World War I, Sir Robert Baden-Powell, the founding father of the Boy Scout movement, became president of the Camping Club of Great

Britain and Ireland. This fostered the establishment of camping organizations in a number of western European countries with the establishment of the Fédération Internationale de Camping et de Caravanning (FICC), in 1932, and the first international camp and congress, which was held in 1933.

The rapid rise in the popularity of camping led to entrepreneurs grabbing up parcels of land with great scenery. They provided organized facilities and camp sites for all campers whatever shape or form they arrived in, including cyclists with their tents, hikers, and backpackers, or people in cars and caravans. The love affair with nature really took off and it seemed like everybody was camping. Friends and families would travel from camp site to camp site to meet regularly under the banner of their clubs for elaborate get-togethers, barbecues, dances, and parties and there were organized events for children. A great deal of development took place in beauty spots for people who wanted to live closer to nature all year round.

Many purists enjoy getting away from it all in remote places, away from other people, and communing in solitary peace with nature. But there are still millions who prefer safety in numbers and submit themselves to the organizational skills of clubs, to enjoy their own forms of camping and their own relationship with the great outdoors.

"The spot was singularly wild and impressive. A wooded amphitheatre, surrounded on three sides by precipitous cliffs of naked granite, sloped gently toward the crest of another precipice that overlooked the valley."

FRANCIS BRET HARTE
The Outcasts of Poker Flat

The Little Bush Maid

by

MARY GRANT BRUCE

"About that fishing excursion, Norah?"

"Yes, Daddy." A small brown paw slid itself into Mr. Linton's hand.

They were sitting on the verandah in the stillness of an autumn evening, watching the shadows on the lawn become vague and indistinct, and finally merge into one haze of dusk. Mr. Linton had been silent for a long time. Norah always knew when her father wanted to talk. This evening she was content to be silent, too, leaning against his knee in her own friendly fashion as she curled up at his feet.

"Oh, you hadn't forgotten, then?"

"Well—not much! Only I didn't know if you really wanted to go, Daddy."

"Why, yes," said her father. "I think it would be rather a good idea, my girlie. There's not much doing on the place just now. I could easily be spared. And we don't want to leave our trip until the days grow shorter. The moon will be right, too. It will be full in four or five days—I forget the exact date. So, altogether, Norah, I think we'd better consult Brownie about the commissariat department, and make our arrangements to go immediately."

"It'll be simply lovely," said his daughter, breathing a long sigh of delight. "Such a long time since we had a camping out—just you and me, Daddy."

"Yes, it's a good while. Well, we've got to make up for lost time by catching plenty of fish," said Mr. Linton. "I hope you haven't forgotten the whereabouts of that fine new hole of yours? You'll have to take me to it if Anglers' Bend doesn't come up to expectations."

...This time there was no "racing and chasing o'er Cannobie Lea" on the way to Anglers' Bend. Mr. Linton's days of scurrying were over, he said, unless a bullock happened to have a difference of opinion as to the way he should go, and, as racing by one's self is a poor thing Norah was content to ride along steadily by her father's side, with only an occasional canter, when Bobs pulled and reefed as if he were as anxious to gallop as his young mistress could possibly be. It was time for lunch when they at length arrived at the well-remembered bend on the creek.

The horses were unsaddled and hobbled, and then turned out to wander at their own sweet will—the shortness of the hobbles a guarantee that they would not stray very far; and the three wanderers sat on the bank of the creek, very ready for the luncheon Mrs. Brown had carefully prepared and placed near the top of the pack. This despatched, preparations were made for pitching camp.

Here luck favored them, for a visit to their former camping place showed that tent poles and pegs were ☞

☜ still there, and uninjured, which considerably lessened the labor of pitching the tents. In a very short time the two tents were standing, and a couple of stretchers rigged up with bags—Mr. Linton had no opinion of the comfort of sleeping on beds of leaves. While her father and Billy were at this work, Norah unpacked the cooking utensils and provisions. Most of the latter were encased in calico bags, which could be hung in the shade, secure from either ants or flies, the remainder, packed in tins, being stowed away easily in the corner of one of the tents.

When the stretchers were ready Norah unpacked the bedding and made their beds. Finally she hung the toothbrushes to the ridge poles and said contentedly, "Daddy, it's just like home!"

"Glad you think so!" said Mr. Linton, casting an approving eye over the comfortable-looking camp, and really there is something wonderfully homelike about a well-pitched camp with a few arrangements for comfort. "At any rate, I think we'll manage very well for a few days, Norah. Now, while Billy lays in a stock of firewood and fixes up a 'humpy' for himself to sleep in, suppose you and I go down and try to catch some fish for tea?"

"Plenty!" laughed Norah.

It soon became evident that Anglers' Bend was going to maintain its name as a place for fish. Scarcely was Norah's line in the water before a big blackfish was on the hook, and after that the fun was fast and furious, until they had caught enough for two or three meals. The day was ideal for fishing—grey and warm, with just enough breeze to ripple the water faintly. Mr. Linton and Norah found it very peaceful, sitting together on the old log that jutted across the stream, and the time passed quickly. Billy at length appeared, and was given the fish to prepare, and then father and daughter returned to camp. Mr. Linton lit the fire, and cutting two stout forked stakes, which he drove into the ground, one on each side of the fire, he hung a green ti-tree pole across, in readiness to hold the billy and frying-pan. Billy presently came up with the fish, and soon a cheery sound of sizzling smote the evening air. By the time that Norah had "the table set," as she phrased it, the fish were ready, and in Norah's opinion no meal ever tasted half so good.

After it was over, Billy the indispensable removed the plates and washed up, and Norah and her father sat by the fire and "yarned" in the cool dusk. Not for long, for soon the little girl began to feel sleepy after the full day in the open air, and the prospect of the comfortable stretcher in her tent was very tempting. She brushed her hair outside in the moonlight, because a small tent is not the place in which to wield a hairbrush; then she slipped into bed, and her father came and tucked her up before tying the flap securely enough to keep out possible intruders in the shape of "bears" and 'possums.

Campfire Cocoa

If you are hiking from campsite to campsite, then you'll want to keep the weight of the equipment you are carrying to a minimum. In which case, you can bring perfectly adequate, ready-made, just-add-hot-water-type hot chocolate powder. Or, you can experiment with flavor at home, making up a dry mix of good cocoa powder, sugar, and dried milk. When satisfied with the taste, make up a container based on those ingredient quantities.

Early settlers probably took milk straight from one of their cows, brought it back to the fire, and made this soothing drink as they pioneered their way across America. Cheer everyone up after a hard day with this authentic recipe.

Cocoa Recipe

MAKES 2 MUGS

> $2\frac{1}{2}$ cups/600ml milk
> $5\frac{1}{2}$ oz/150g bittersweet chocolate, cut up
> $\frac{2}{3}$ cup/150ml heavy cream
> unsweetened cocoa powder for dusting

1. Heat the milk in a pan to just below boiling. Stir in the chocolate pieces until melted. Pour into mugs.
2. Whip the cream until barely stiff, then float on top of the cocoa. Dust with cocoa powder.

"Blow, bugle, blow, set the wild echoes flying…"

ALFRED, LORD TENNYSON

Girl Scouts

The year 1910 was an important one for girls, almost coming about by accident and certainly by a happy coincidence. That summer in the Vermont town of Thetford, William Chauncy Langdon organized a community play involving a number of boy scouts to celebrate the town's 150th anniversary. The girls of the town, who had no organization specifically for them, asked if they might also be involved, so Langdon leveled up the playing field by forming what he called The Camp Fire Girls. Like the Boy Scouts, The Camp Fire Girls had levels of achievement to strive for, which were Wood Gatherer, Fire Maker, and Torch Bearer. The leader of the group was titled the Guardian of the Fire.

Meanwhile, over in Maine, Dr. Luther Halsey Gulick and his wife, Charlotte, ran a summer camp for girls, just as they had done over the years for their own daughters. Only now there were 17 others joining them at Lake Sebago to hike, swim, play sports, do craftwork, cook out, and sing around the campfire. The girls, seeking a name for their camp, asked Mrs. Gulick who, taking the first two letters from the words "work," "health," and "love" came up with Camp Wohelo. The girls all chose personal names from Native American languages that in someway represented the kind of person they hoped to become, and they designed a fringed brown cotton uniform for themselves onto which they added Native American designs and motifs. At their campfire meetings they would receive beads and emblems for their achievements.

The Gulicks and William Langdon brought their ideas together with a view to creating an organization that could exist nationwide. Soon after, in 1912, The Camp Fire Girls, Inc. was born. It swiftly caught the nation's imagination with more than 60,000 members joining in the first year alone. It became the talk of the media and was taken up in more than 40 states with girls adopting much of the ceremony and activities that the small group of girls had undertaken at Camp Wohelo.

The popularity of the organization spread rapidly with a little help from the onslaught of Camp Fire Girl adventure stories that were published the same year, starting with Irene Elliott Benson's *How Ethel Hollister Became a Campfire Girl*. There followed a great many titles on similar subject matter, penned by numerous authors and as one of them, Elizabeth Duffield expressed in her introduction to *Lucile, the Torch Bearer* (1915):

"The organization of Camp Fire Girls, although of recent origin, has had an astonishing growth and bids fair to rival the Boy Scout movement, with whose aims and ideals it has many things in common.... The Camp Fire is the symbol of the happy, outdoor life with its wholesome activities....Nothing but good can come from such an organization...."

EXTRACT FROM

Camp Fire Girls: In the Woods

by

JANE L. STEWART

Bessie came first, and Wanaka turned to her.

"Is it your desire to become a Camp Fire Girl and follow the law of the Fire?"

And Bessie, who had been taught the form to be followed, answered:

"It is my desire to become a Camp Fire Girl and to obey the law of the Camp Fire, which is to Seek Beauty, Give Service, Pursue Knowledge, Be Trustworthy, Hold on to Health, Glorify Work, Be Happy. This law of the Camp Fire I will strive to follow."

Then she held out her left hand, and Eleanor took it, saying:

"In the name of the Camp Fire Girls of America, I place on the little finger of your left hand this ring, with its design of seven fagots, symbolic of the seven points of the law of the Fire, which you have expressed your desire to follow, and of the three circles on either side, symbolic of the three watchwords of this organization—Work, Health, and Love. And—

"As fagots are brought from the forest
Firmly held by the sinews which bind them,

So cleave to these others, your sisters,
Wherever, whenever, you find them.
"Be strong as the fagots are sturdy;
Be pure in your deepest desire;
Be true to the truth that is in you;
And—follow the law of the Fire."

Then, as Bessie, or Stella, as, at the Council Fire she was to be known thereafter, made her way back to her place, all the girls sang the Wo-he-lo song by way of welcoming her as one of them.

Barbecue Chicken

SERVES 4

1 chicken or 12 chicken pieces,

For the barbecue sauce:
1 tbsp olive oil
1 onion, chopped
2 garlic cloves, finely chopped
1 small (8oz/200g) can diced tomatoes
5 tbsp tomato paste
3½ fl oz/100ml beer
1 tbsp honey or brown sugar
1-2 tbsp Worcestershire sauce
1 bay leaf
½ tsp crushed chili flakes
1 tsp dried thyme
2 tsp lemon juice

For the dry marinade:
1 tsp salt
1 tsp pepper
12 tsp cayenne
2 garlic cloves, crushed
1 tsp mustard powder

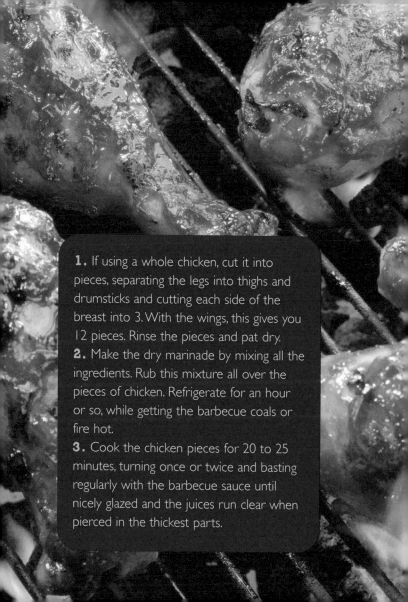

1. If using a whole chicken, cut it into pieces, separating the legs into thighs and drumsticks and cutting each side of the breast into 3. With the wings, this gives you 12 pieces. Rinse the pieces and pat dry.

2. Make the dry marinade by mixing all the ingredients. Rub this mixture all over the pieces of chicken. Refrigerate for an hour or so, while getting the barbecue coals or fire hot.

3. Cook the chicken pieces for 20 to 25 minutes, turning once or twice and basting regularly with the barbecue sauce until nicely glazed and the juices run clear when pierced in the thickest parts.

O twilight hour of dreams!
Rest, bare feet, by my lake of glass,
Where the mirrored sunset gleams.

KATHARINE LEE BATES
"A Song of Riches"

World Famous Song

"Ging Gang Gooli" came about during the first World Jamboree when Baden-Powell was looking for a song that everyone, regardless of their language could sing together. The song that resulted was a great hit and has remained a classic for scouts all over the world to this day. Even though it has no actual meaning, there is a tale that is often told about how it originated, that goes something like this:

In deepest, darkest Africa there is a famous legend concerning the Great Gray Ghost Elephant. It is said that every year, after the rains, the Great Gray Ghost Elephant would rise from the mists and wander the land at dawn. At villages, he would stop, sniff, and then either walk around the village or through it. If he went around the village, the people of the village would have a prosperous year; if he went through it, hunger and drought would follow.

The village of Wat-Cha had already been visited three years in a row by the elephant. The village leader, Ging-Ganga, was very worried, as was the village medicine man Hay-la-shay. They decided to do something about the problem. Ging-Ganga and his warriors were to stand in the path of the elephant when it came and shake their shields and spears at it to frighten it away. Hay-la-shay and his followers would cast magic spells to deter the elephant by shaking their medicine bags, which made a loud "shalawally, shalawally, shalawally" sound when shaken.

The villagers took their places, Ging-Ganga and his warriors on one side, and Hay-la-shay and his followers on the other. As they waited, the warriors sang softly about their leader:

"Ging gang gooli, gooli, gooli, gooli, watcha, Ging, gang goo, Ging, gang goo, Ging gang gooli, gooli, gooli, gooli, watcha, Ging, gang goo, Ging, gang goo."

And the medicine men sang of their leader:

"Heyla, heyla sheyla, Heyla sheyla, heyla ho, Heyla, heyla sheyla, Heyla sheyla, heyla ho."

And then they shook their medicine bags:

"Shalli-walli, shalli-walli, Shalli-walli, shalli-walli."

And from the river came the mighty Great Gray Ghost Elephant's call:

"Oompa, oompa, oompa ..."

The elephant came closer, and the warriors beat their shields and sang louder: 👉

👉 "Ging gang gooli, gooli, gooli, gooli, watcha, Ging, gang goo, Ging, gang goo, Ging gang gooli, gooli, gooli, gooli, watcha, Ging, gang goo, Ging, gang goo."

Then the medicine men rose and sang as loud they were able:

"Heyla, heyla sheyla, Heyla sheyla, heyla ho, Heyla, heyla sheyla, Heyla sheyla, heyla ho."

And they shook their medicine bags with all their might:

"Shalli-walli, shalli-walli, Shalli-walli, shalli-walli."

And the mighty Great Gray Ghost Elephant turned aside and went around the village, saying:

"Oompa, oompa, oompa …"

There was great rejoicing in the village and all the villagers joined in to sing their new celebratory song.

Ging Gang Gooli

Ging gang gooli, gooli, gooli, gooli, watcha,
Ging, gang goo, Ging, gang goo,
Ging gang gooli, gooli, gooli, gooli, watcha,
Ging, gang goo, Ging, gang goo.

Heyla, heyla sheyla,
Heyla sheyla, heyla ho,
Heyla, heyla sheyla,
Heyla sheyla, heyla ho.

Shalli-walli, shalli-walli, Shalli-walli, shalli-walli.

Oompa, oompa, oompa…

First Aid

When man leaves the familiar territory of his everyday existence and sets about exploring and communing with nature, he leaves himself open to the unforeseen, which can sometimes have the unfortunate result of accident or injury.

It is, therefore, a wise group of campers who make certain that they know what to do should the worst happen and they need to apply first aid.

The first rule should always be accident prevention, and simple common sense should always prevail. When working with and around open fires, always take precautions to avoid being burned. Never keep bedding close to the fire, always lift hot pots with oven mitts, and move logs using tongs. If you don't have tongs, a basic pair can be made using two long greenish sticks that are naturally curved, one with a forked end. Lay them together so the stems are curved against each other, and bind them in a sprung-open position.

Never dive into water because you could fracture your skull or injure your neck on submerged rocks. In the worst case, you could be left permanently paralyzed. A common injury in hot countries, the lure of cool, refreshing water tempts far too many to risk their necks by taking a dive.

Never poke around in places where wild animals might be hiding. Snakes may be poisonous and nesting bees, wasps, or hornets may become agitated and attack. Keep well away.

Protect your feet from blisters when hiking by wearing good boots and clean, dry socks. Keep your feet clean, and always dry your feet well after they have been in water. Treat cuts, stings, and abrasions with antiseptic and apply bandages to keep dirt out of open wounds. In tropical climates, sores and cuts can easily fester and turn septic, so it is wise to carry antiseptic powder.

Always wash your hands thoroughly before handling food, after handling uncooked meat, and, of course, after toilet usage. A stomach upset in the wilderness is a particularly unpleasant experience.

Beware of touching plants and flowers in the wild. Many possess chemical properties that can seriously irritate your skin and eyes. Do not eat anything from the wilderness that you are not absolutely certain of. Many toadstools and berries look delicious but are actually highly poisonous.

Always have an appropriate supply of materials in your first-aid kit:

Assorted Band-Aids

Antiseptic solution

Alcohol-free wipes

Alcohol wipes

Insect repellent wipes

Burn relief gel

Low adherent absorbent pad

    2 x 2in/5 x 5cm ☞

IN CAMP

FIRST-AID

☜ Pack of cotton swabs
Scalpel blade
First-aid information sheet
Safety pins
Surgical gloves
Antihistamine tablets
Diarrhea tablets
Foil heat-retaining blanket
Tweezers
Magnifying glass
Plastic strip thermometer
Instant cold pack (for heat
    exhaustion and as a cold
    treatment for burns,
    bruises, sprains, swelling,
    headaches, and toothaches)
Water-sterilization kit
Medical tape
Needle and thread
Scissors

Eye dressing (sticks poking in
    the eye are very common)
Elastic wrap bandage
Triangular bandage (for
    injured arms and
    shoulders)
Large compression bandage
Lip balm (with sun protection)
Adult pain reliever
Children's pain reliever
Salt tablets (for hot climates)
Calamine lotion (for poison
    oak, poison ivy,
    or poison sumac)
Eye drops
Bandages for blisters
Antiseptic foot powder
Sunscreen
A thin sterile tube to make
    an artificial airway

The list could go on and on, but try not to overload your
backpack. You don't want to be weighed down by large amounts
of equipment when hiking. ☞

☞ WHEN THE WORST HAPPENS

It takes very little to turn a camping trip into a survival situation. Imagine a father out on a hike, ten miles from civilization with a couple of children in tow—the unforeseen happens and the father trips and breaks his leg. This is where it is not only good but vital for the youngsters to be trained in first aid. Everyone should know how to deal with basic injuries and disorders, and it takes a particular courage to make life-saving decisions.

It's best for all campers to take a first-aid course, or at the very least, to take a first-aid book on any camping trip. Outlined below are the main, basic first-aid skills that every camper should know.

PRIORITIES

- **Restore the breathing and heartbeat if it has stopped, and maintain it**
- **Stop the bleeding**
- **Protect the wounds or burns**
- **Immobilize any fractures**
- **Treat the shock** ☞

☜ WHAT IS ARTIFICIAL RESPIRATION?

This is also known as the Kiss of Life or mouth-to-mouth resuscitation, but its official name is cardiopulmonary resuscitation (CPR). Before you start, be prepared to continue for quite a while. Lie the patient flat on their back, hold the jaw well open with one hand, and tilt the head back. Pinch the patient's nose with your other hand, clear their mouth of all obstructions, and place your mouth over the patient's mouth. Exhale into them, watching for their chest to rise, then remove your mouth and take a deep breath as their chest falls again. Repeat the process as quickly as possible for the first six breaths and continue to administer at least 12 breaths per minute. Keep going and check their heartbeat.

If there is no pulse, start cardiac compressions while continuing artificial respiration. You must not lose any time here. With the patient on a firm surface, lie them chest facing upward and use the edge of the hand to strike firmly on the lower part of the breastbone, which may jar the heart into restarting. If you still can't find a pulse, then begin the compressions or external cardiac massage. While kneeling by the patient, place the heel of one hand on the lower half of the breastbone, which is that central bone between the ribs. Not at the end of it or below it, but low down on it. Place the other hand on top of the first hand and with straight arms rock yourself forward and press down six to eight times for every lungful of air you provide. If you are in a group these tasks can be shared out, otherwise you will have to cope alone giving a repeated pattern of 15 heart compressions to two rapid lung inflations. Keep checking for a return of the pulse.

Remain positive and persist. Once breathing and pulse are restored, place your patient in the recovery position (see page 241) and monitor regularly.

BLEEDING

When blood loss is great, the flow must be stopped as soon as possible because blood carries oxygen. The lost blood is made up from fluids drawn from the body's tissues. Vein and capillary bleeds can be stemmed by applying pressure over the bleeding point. Minor arterial bleeding can also be dealt with in a similar way. Use the cleanest materials available, and apply firm pressure as quickly as possible. Maintain the pressure for up to ten minutes, which should stop the bleeding. Keep placing new pads on top of each old one until blood stops seeping through. Once in control, bandage the pads to the wound to keep the pressure maintained.

You'll be amazed how quickly you can learn to save not only your own life, but those of others around you—people you love, who might someday depend on you to survive. 🖘

☜ CHOKING

Should the patient be unconscious, be prepared to give
CPR (see page 238). Lie them down flat on their back and
kneel astride them placing one hand upon the other and
with the heels of the palms resting just above the navel,
make several quick thrusts up to the center of the ribcage.
If the blockage still doesn't clear, roll the patient onto their
side and strike four times between their shoulder blades,
repeating as necessary. In most cases obstructions will clear
early in these procedures. There is always hope in a life-or-
death situation, as long as you persevere and create an
emergency artificial airway.

Anyone is susceptible to choking and it can often be resolved
using the Heimlich maneuver. Reassure the patient by swiftly
taking a position behind them. Place your arms around them
as though you're hugging them from behind. With one hand
make a clenched fist and place the thumb side of your fist
against the upper abdomen, below the ribcage, and above
the navel. Grab your fist with your free hand and apply
firm pressure, jerking your hands upward four times in
quick succession. If this proves unsuccessful the first time,
deliver four sharp blows to the back between the shoulder
blades, which may loosen the object, and then repeat the
Heimlich maneuver.

UNCONSCIOUS

Check to see if the injured camper is breathing. If not then commence CPR immediately. This act should be maintained while searching for any external bleeding or other reasons for unconsciousness.

CONSCIOUS

If the patient is breathing, and providing they show no signs of spinal injury, move them with extreme care. If there is spinal damage, the injured should not be moved, unless it is absolutely life threatening to leave them where they are. If there is no spinal injury, check their mouth for any obstruction, and place them in the recovery position by turning the patient on their side. Lift their chin forward to open the airways and adjust their hand under their cheek as necessary. Make sure that they can not roll forward or backward (see diagram). Loosen their clothing and pull the jaw outward a little, which will ensure the tongue is not blocking their airway.

The Outdoor Chums

by

CAPTAIN QUINCY ALLEN

The horses had not had a very hard pull up to this time, and were, therefore, in pretty fair condition to attempt the last quarter of the journey... After rather a trying experience they finally sighted a column of smoke, and, calling Toby's attention to this, Frank said:

"That's as far as we go this time, Toby."

Toby shut his eyes for a brief moment and doubtless gave thanks, for his poor old body must have been pretty well bruised by this time.

Will and Bluff had spied the wagon by now, and they shouted a noisy welcome.

"Now we're prepared for a siege, with the grub at hand," cried Bluff, dancing around with his gun held on high.

"Say, be careful with that contraption, will you? If ever it started going off not one of us would live to tell the ghastly tale," called Will, as if really and truly alarmed, which, of course, he was not.

Bluff gave him an indignant look, for it pained him to have his pet gun insulted after this rude fashion; but he was too much delighted over the coming of the supply wagon to cherish any animosity; and besides, as

Frank said, he never could keep on being angry over a few minutes at a time.

Such fun they had getting that vehicle unloaded.

Then the tents had to go up, which was an operation that consumed considerable time, for Frank proved to be very exact in his way of arranging things, and would not accept any poor work.

When finally both tents had been erected, with a burgee bearing the club name floating from the very tops, the camp began to have a mighty cheery look that was invigorating.

Then another fly was put up just in the rear, under which some of the coarser provisions, such as water would not injure should the rain get in, were stored; here, too, Toby was to bunk while in camp.

"Everything looks like business, boys," said Jerry, as he came in later.

"What did you do with Erastus?" demanded Frank; "upset him in a ditch?"

"Do I look like I had been rooting? He got off on the train, and is home by now."

Home—the boys looked at each other, for it already seemed as though they had been away a long time, and yet their first night under canvas was still ahead.

They meant to keep the horses with them over night, and next day Jerry would go with Toby to the farmer's, about a mile off, leaving the outfit there until it was needed to take them back again.

…The unusual exertions of the ride and subsequent ☞

☞ wood-chopping had really tired all of the chums, though none of them would publicly admit it. When Bluff attempted to get up in a hurry for some purpose, he found himself so stiff he could hardly move, and it was only after much grunting and three distinct efforts that he finally managed to reach his feet.

Frank only smiled.

He had expected just this, and knew that in a few days the boys would have succeeded in getting the kinks out of their muscles.

Bluff had insisted that they have fried onions with that glorious steak, and, indeed, he even prepared a dozen of the same himself, for Bluff could be very persistent when he chose; Frank called a halt at this number.

"We may want a few another time, old fellow," he admonished.

"Oh! all right, then. I was just waiting till somebody called me off. I've shed more tears than Brutus ever dropped at the bier of Caesar. Wow! Some kind person wipe my eyes, please; my hands are too rank to touch my tear-rag," he declared, and Will performed this friendly office, thinking that he deserved it after his heroism.

The coffee was soon bubbling on the fire, and the delightful odor of that fine sirloin steak, together with a second frying-pan full of onions, so permeated the surrounding atmosphere that had any of the Lasher crowd been hiding in the vicinity they must have suffered tortures in the thought that they were debarred from that glorious outdoor feast around the first campfire.

"Look there!" said Jerry, quietly, pointing as he spoke.

"It's a little chipmunk come to find out what all this row is about here," remarked Frank, tossing a piece of bread toward the cunning animal. "If you don't do anything to frighten them away we can have a lot of such friendly creatures hanging around the camp all the time."

"Then, for goodness' sake, chain up that annihilator of Bluff's before he gets it working overtime. Looks as if he had an eye on it just now, for game is game to the pot hunter, no matter how he gets it, or what it happens to be," growled Jerry, scowling in the direction of the other, who only grinned in reply.

"Supper am ready, gemmen. Kindly draw yer seats 'round de table," announced the tow-headed cook at this juncture; and in the eagerness to appease their keen hunger everything else was forgotten for the time being.

Two collapsible tables had been brought along, and these were placed under the raised fly of one of the tents, so that the warmth of the open fire could be enjoyed; but the whole supper had not been cooked after the old fashion, for Frank had a little outfit that burned kerosene, making its own blue flame, and which the other boys declared to be the finest thing of the kind they had ever seen.

Etiquette and Environment

Throughout the world recreational land, including privately owned land and national parkland, is being enjoyed by more and more people who come to visit and use it for hiking, camping, and backpacking. The sheer scale of the increase in usage is frightening considering that if you multiply each hiker who ventures off the trail, or each group that creates a new campsite of their own by millions, there will be an inevitable, substantial accumulative effect on the land.

Trampling off track causes a loss of vegetation, changes in species composition, exposure, compaction, and erosion of soil, and damage to trees. Add to the equation the campfire scars, improperly disposed of litter, human and pet waste, and things begin to escalate out of control. They don't only ruin the land, they ruin camping and outdoor activities for everyone.

The constant increase in the amount of human disturbance to wildlife displaces animals from critical foraging, nesting, and mating. Problems have already become widespread where wildlife has started to beg from humans. This is not only bad for animals, but a nuisance and potential danger to us.

The challenge is to eliminate all avoidable impact and to minimize the unavoidable impact of our commune with nature. It is up to every camper to modify their own behavior and set examples for others to follow if we are to continue to enjoy access to the natural world.

There is a code of practice that can be adopted, based on the principle of leaving no trace of our ever having been there. Much is common sense, and there is no reason in the world why campers shouldn't adhere to the principles and still have a rewarding, enjoyable time in the wilderness.

- **Always** plan ahead and prepare
- **Wherever** possible travel and camp only on durable surfaces, such as established trails, and campsites, rock, gravel, dry grasses, or snow
- **Dispose** of waste properly
- **Leave** what you find
- **Minimize** the impacts of any campfire
- **Respect** wildlife and leave it alone
- **Be** considerate of other visitors. A boozy, loud group can destroy the peace for many and lead to conflict
- **Always** familiarize yourself with the regulations and special concerns of the area you visit
- **Be** prepared for extreme weather, hazards, and emergencies
- **Try** to avoid visits at times of high usage
- **Visit** in smaller parties or split up your larger groups into no more than six people
- **Repackage** food to minimize waste ☞

☞

- **Use** a map and compass to eliminate the use of marking paint, rock cairns, or flagging
- **Camp** at least 200ft/61m from lakes and streams.
- **Find** a campsite, don't forge your own. Altering existing sites is not necessary
- **Use** existing trails
- **Walk** single file in the middle of a trail, even when the pathway is wet or muddy
- **Keep** campsites small and focus human activity on areas where vegetation is absent
- **Pack** out everything you pack in
- **Inspect** your campsite and rest area for trash or spilled foods before leaving
- **Dispose** of all trash, leftover food, and litter. Deposit solid human waste in cat holes, dug 6–8in/10–15cm deep at least 200ft/61m from water, camp, and trails. Cover and disguise the cat hole when finished
- **Dispose** of toilet paper and hygiene products
- **To** wash yourself or your dishes, carry water 200ft/61m away from streams or lakes and use small amounts of biodegradable soap or grit. Scatter strained dishwater
- **Preserve** the past. Examine and explore but do not touch cultural or historic structures and certainly never artifacts
- **Leave** rocks, plants, and other natural objects as you find them

- **Never** introduce or transport nonnative species
- **Do** not build structures, furniture, or dig trenches except where permitted
- **Minimize** campfire impact and consider using a lightweight stove for cooking. Enjoy a candle lantern for light as an alternative
- **Where** fires are permitted, use established fire rings, fire pans, or mound fires
- **Keep** fires small. Only use sticks from the ground that can be broken by hand. Burn all wood and coals to ash, put out campfires completely, and then scatter cool ashes
- **Observe** wildlife from a distance. Never stalk or approach wild animals
- **Never** feed animals. Feeding wildlife damages their health and alters their natural behaviors, which could expose them to predators and other dangers
- **Protect** wildlife and your food by storing rations and trash securely
- **Control** pets at all times, or better still, leave them at home
- **Be** sensitive to wildlife during times of mating, nesting, raising young, or during the winter
- **Respect** other visitors and protect the quality of their experience as much as your own
- **Be** courteous. Yield to other campers on the trail

How to Make Quick Shelters

Imagine that you need to take shelter quickly from the wind or the rain, and you have no equipment with you. Look around and see what natural protection is nearby. Try and find a rock face, a gradient, or whatever is available in nature that can be incorporated to make your shelter more protective.

People have it within themselves to be quite ingenious when it comes to surviving and creating shelter where none seems apparent. Many people, for example, have perished while walking through snow-covered pine forests, unable to see the wood for the trees. In emergency circumstances, it would be best to find a big bushy conifer and cut halfway through its trunk, about 3ft/91cm from the ground. Then lay it over so that it remains hinged to its trunk, forming a wedge-shaped slope to the ground. Cut or tear out the inner pine branches and weave them into the outside branches. This creates a good hollowed-out shelter. A layer of pine needle branches laid across the ground makes an effective barrier against damp vegetation. Once sheltered from the wind, rain, or snow, it's much easier to concentrate on building a fire.

Armed with just a sheet of plastic it's possible to make all kinds of effective shelters. The following tents and shelters can be erected quickly in an emergency with the minimum amount of equipment.

MAKE A SAPLING SHELTER:

Prepare two lines of saplings—
about four either side.

Bind them together
at the tops to create
a sort of bowed tunnel.
Run one along the length
at the top to lash them all
together and stop sideward
movement. (See fig. 1)

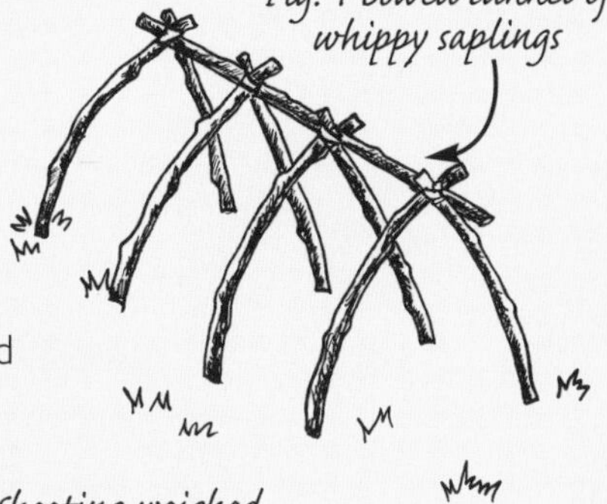

Fig. 1 Bowed tunnel of whippy saplings

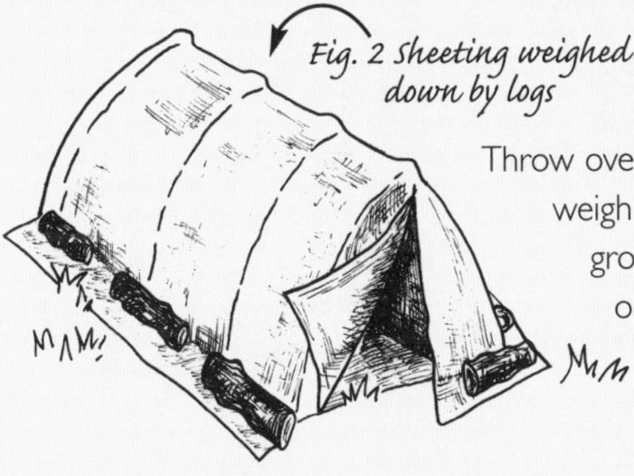

Fig. 2 Sheeting weighed down by logs

Throw over your sheeting and
weigh the edges down at
ground level using logs
or stones. (See fig. 2)

Bigger versions of these are very similar to what the Gypsies
used to call bender tents—shelters that resembled the backs
of old-fashioned covered wagons.

MAKE A DOMED SAPLING SHELTER:

Another good version along the same lines, which will provide more room, is a dome structure. Lash whippy saplings together at the top, and sink their bottoms into the ground. (See fig. 3)

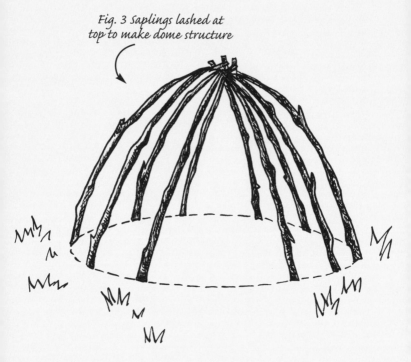

Fig. 3 Saplings lashed at top to make dome structure

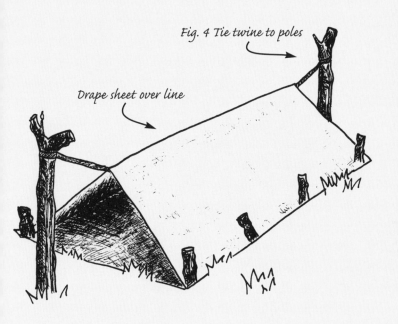

Fig. 4 Tie twine to poles

Drape sheet over line

MAKE A SIMPLE TENT:

Armed with only sheeting and a length of twine, it's possible to make a wide range of shelters that will keep campers out of harm's way. Find two upright poles about 4½ft/1.4m long. Drive them into the ground in line, about 7ft/2m apart. Tie twine to one, and then stretch it and tie it to the top of the other. Spread sheeting out over the line, and angle it out to make a tent shape. Weigh down the edges with stones or wood. (See fig. 4)

Fig. 5 Double layer of sheeting

MAKE A DOUBLE LAYERED TENT:

Less waterproof materials, such as spare blankets, can be put to use as a tent. If the sheets are double layered, then the water that gets through one layer will slow down and often not get through to the second. Construct the framework of the shelter in the same way as for fig. 4. However, tie another length of twine between the upright poles directly above the first length and drape a second sheet over it. (See fig. 5)

MAKE A WEDGE-SHAPED TENT:

In very windy conditions, create a wedge-shaped shelter with its apex facing into the wind. (See fig. 6)

Always ensure you have a good spread of bedding in the form of soft pine branches or bracken. Lying on the cold damp ground is likely to leave you very sick.

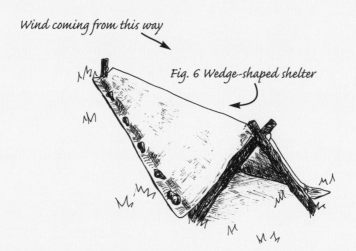

Wind coming from this way

Fig. 6 Wedge-shaped shelter

It is always fun to experiment with the construction of shelters and it makes for good playtime as well.

With my saddle all shedded and the cattle all bedded
Nothing wild seems to be wrong;
Make my bed 'neath the skies,
I look up at the stars,
And then I can sing you this call.

TEX RITTER
"Cattle Call"

Waltzing Matilda

BY ANDREW BARTON "BANJO" PATTERSON, C.1890

Once a jolly swagman camped by a billabong,
Under the shade of a coolabah tree,
And he sang as he watched and waited till his billy boiled
You'll come a waltzing Matilda with me.

Waltzing Matilda, Waltzing Matilda,
You'll come a waltzing Matilda with me,
And he sang as he watched and waited till his billy boiled,
You'll come a waltzing Matilda with me.

Down came a jumbuck to drink at that billabong,
Up jumped the swagman and grabbed him with glee,
And he sang as he shoved that jumbuck in his tucker-bag
You'll come a waltzing Matilda with me.

Waltzing Matilda, Waltzing Matilda,
You'll come a waltzing Matilda with me,
And he sang as he shoved that jumbuck in his tucker-bag,
You'll come a waltzing Matilda with me.

Up rode the squatter mounted on his thoroughbred,
Down came the troopers—one, two, three,
Whose that jolly jumbuck you've got in your tucker-bag?
You'll come a waltzing Matilda with me.

Waltzing Matilda, Waltzing Matilda,
You'll come a waltzing Matilda with me,
Whose that jolly jumbuck you've got in your tucker-bag?
You'll come a waltzing Matilda with me.

Up jumped the swagman, and sprang
    into the billabong,
You'll never catch me alive said he,
And his ghost may be heard as you
    pass by that billabong
You'll come a waltzing Matilda with me.

Waltzing Matilda, Waltzing Matilda,
You'll come a waltzing Matilda with me,
And his ghost may be heard as you pass
    by that billabong,
You'll come a waltzing Matilda with me.

Explorers and Trappers

Camping today is a peaceful and relatively safe pastime that owes much to the perilous journeys of the pioneers and explorers who were faced with long, exhausting treks into the unknown. Some sought a better life, and others were driven by the spirit of adventure. A few became great characters of legend. Such was the buckskin-clad hunter, trapper, and pioneer Daniel Boone, who was born in Pennsylvania in 1734. He spent part of his life living on the North Carolina frontier, hunting and trapping, and was known to have trekked as far south as Florida. Boone, often depicted in a beaver-skin hat, was captured twice by Native Americans during his time in Kentucky, but each time he escaped. However, he liked Kentucky so much he settled there as the founding father and protector of Boonesboro.

Many people get confused between Boone and Davy Crockett (see pages 180–181), another fine example of a nineteenth-century frontiersman, who was also a businessman and politician.

James Bowie was another folk hero from Kentucky and was quite the entrepreneur. Born in 1796 and venturing out in life at the age of 18 he set his sights on property speculation with its sidelines of land clearance and timber. He was also involved in slave-trading and sugar plantations. In the Texas Revolution of 1835–1836 Bowie was one of the leading participants at the Battle of Concepcion and was known for being a reckless adventurer. He also became famous for using a type of hunting knife, which became widely known as the Bowie Knife—it has remained the benchmark for knife-makers to this day. But ultimately, he too lost his life at the Battle of the Alamo.

The capital city of Nevada was named after yet another historical character. Christopher "Kit" Carson, born in 1809 started out as an apprentice to a saddler and become an explorer, hunter, trapper, frontiersman, scout, Indian agent, and soldier. His experience was forged on the infamous Santa Fe Trail. Carson was known to speak a number of languages fluently, including Spanish, Navajo, Apache, Cheyenne, and many more. He became very popular when authors who wrote wild adventure stories about the American West chose to write about him. These "dime novels" (they cost ten cents) were mainly exaggerated and fictionalized versions of real events.

Then came the legendary Sam Houston whose name was the inspiration for the largest city in Texas. A curious figure of a man, Houston was torn between the two worlds of the white man's Texas and the Cherokee nation that adopted him. He went on to become the President of the Republic of Texas for eight years and later became a U.S. senator when Texas joined the union.

To my lone heart the prairie springs

HAMLIN GARLAND

"To a Captive Crane"

The Swiss Family Robinson

by

JOHANN DAVID WYSS

We were all up at the break of day, and knelt down to thank God that He had kept us from harm through the night. We then put all the things on the raft, and ten live hens and two cocks were put in one of the tubs. Some ducks and geese we let go, in the hope that they would swim to the shore; and a pair of doves were set free, as they could fly to the land. There was a place in the raft for each of us. In the first tub sat my wife; in the next Frank, who was eight years old; in the third Fritz, not quite twice the age of Frank; in the fourth were the fowls, and some old sails that would make us a tent; the fifth was full of good things in the way of food; in the sixth stood Jack, a bold lad, ten years old; in the next Ernest, twelve years of age, well taught, but too fond of self, and less fond of work than the rest; while I sat in the eighth, to guide the raft that was to save all that was dear to me in the world.

As soon as the dogs (Bill and Turk by name) saw us push off from the ship they leaped in the sea, swam near the raft, and kept well up with us. The sea was calm; so that we felt quite safe. We made good use of the oars, and the raft bore its freight straight to the land; but as we drew near to the shore the sight of the bare rocks led us to think that we might still be in need of food and drink when that which we had was gone.

As we got near, the coast lost its bare look, and we were glad to see that there was no lack of trees. We soon found a bay, to which the ducks and geese had found their way, and here we saw a place where we could land.

As soon as we had made the raft fast with a strong rope, we took out all our wealth, and made a tent with the old sail cloth we had brought with us, and stuck a pole in the ground to keep it up. This done, I sent the boys to get some moss and dry grass to make our beds with. With the flint and steel we soon set fire to some dry twigs, and my wife made a pot of soup with what she had brought from the ship. Fritz, who had charge of the guns, chose one, and took a stroll by the side of a stream, while Jack went in search of shellfish, which he thought he might find on the rocks. My share of the work was to save two large casks, which were near the shore. While I was up to my knees in the sea I heard a ☞

shrill cry, which I knew to come from Jack. I got out at once, took up an axe, and ran to his help. I found him with his legs in a rock pool, where a large crab held him by his toes. It soon made off as I came near; but I struck at it with the axe, and brought it out of the pool. Jack then took it up, though it gave him a pinch or two ere he found out how to hold it, and ran off in high glee to show what he had caught.

When I got back to the tent, I found that Ernest had brought us news that he had seen salt in the chinks of the rocks, and that shellfish were not scarce.

"Well, my boy, if you are sure you saw them, I will ask you to go back for some. We must each do some work for the good of all."

He went, and soon found the salt, left by the sea on the rocks, which the sun had made quite dry. There was some sand with it, but my wife did not take long to find a way to cure that. She had been to a fresh stream with a large jug; from this I saw her pour some on the salt, strain it through a cloth, and let it drip in a cup, so that all the sand was left on the cloth.

When the soup was made hot we had each a taste, and all said that it was good.

"Be not in too great haste," said my wife, "we must wait for Fritz; but if he were here, I do not see how we are to take our soup, for we have no plates nor spoons."

"If we had but some large nuts," said Ernest, "we might cut them in half, and they would make good bowls."

"Quite true," said I; "but as there are none, we may as well wish for delf bowls and real spoons at once."

"Now I have it," quoth Ernest. "Let us use the shells I saw on the shore."

Off ran Jack to the shore, with Ernest at his heels, and back they both came with large and small shells for us all.

…We all sat down to take our soup with the shell spoons. Ernest took from his coat a large shell, which he had hid till now, put it in the soup, and then set it down to cool.

"You do not show want of thought," said I to him. "But I am not glad to see that you think so of yourself, and do so much for your own ease, when all the rest do so much for yours. Now, that shell full of soup you must give to our two dogs. We can all dip our small shells in the pot, and you must do as we do."

The Log of a Cowboy

A NARRATIVE OF THE OLD TRAIL DAYS

BY ANDY ADAMS

It proved an ideal camp, with wood, water, and grass in abundance, and very little range stock to annoy us. We had watered the herd just before noon, and before throwing them upon the bed ground for the night, watered them a second time. We had a splendid campfire that night, of dry live oak

logs, and after supper was over and the first guard had taken the herd, smoking and storytelling were the order of the evening. The campfire is to all outdoor life what the evening fireside is to domestic life. After the labors of the day are over, the men gather around the fire, and the social hour of the day is spent in yarning. The stories told may run from the sublime to the ridiculous, from a true incident to a base fabrication, or from a touching bit of pathos to the most vulgar vulgarity.

Sloppy Joes

SERVES 4–6

1 lb/450g minced beef
1 large onion, chopped
1 celery stalk, chopped
1 green pepper, seeded and chopped
4oz/115g mushrooms, sliced
4 tbsp tomato ketchup
2 cups/450ml tomato juice
salt and pepper
2 tsp Tabasco or other chili sauce
   (or more if you wish)
2 tbsp cornstarch
hamburger buns, to serve

1. In a large, dry skillet, brown the meat well all over, breaking up lumps. Stir in the vegetables and continue to cook until they are tender.

2. Add the ketchup and tomato juice with some seasoning and Tabasco sauce to taste, then mix in the cornstarch. Mix well and cook on a very low heat for at least 2 hours, but the longer the better.

3. Serve hot on hamburger buns. If you want, you can toast the buns before filling them.

Always take a good look at what you're about to eat. It's not so important to know what it is, but it's critical to know what it was.

TRADITIONAL COWBOY PROVERB

Cooking Over Wood

SMOKING AND FLAVORING

Cooking over wood can impart the most delicious range of flavors to barbecued or grilled foods. It's important for all good campfire cooks to know how to exploit this possibility to the full. Smoking wood is available from stores in various forms, as wood chips, which are suitable for food with shorter cooking times, and as larger chunks for foods that take longer.

Wood chips can be used in a wood-burning pit, wood-burning grill, or even a gas grill. To use them in a pit, grill, or a gas grill unit, you need a cast-iron smoker box (or you can use a heavy-duty aluminum foil container) to keep them from burning up. Soak them in water or apple juice for at least one hour before using.

The best way to smoke food is on a covered barbecue, but it's much more authentic to scatter the wood among the coals of an open fire. Then, once it's burning well, you can damp it down with a little extra water to create more smoke.

If you're using chunks of wood, be sure to soak them for an hour before using. If you use two or three sticks about 7–15in/17.5–35cm long, let them burn down to a bed of nonflaming coals. They should give you good results and provide a steady source of heat and smoke for you to cook your food over.

When the wood starts smoking, begin grilling, and, if you're cheating and using a portable covered barbecue, keep the lid on. Add more soaked chips when you no longer see smoke coming out of the vents. Try not to overdo the smoking though; you want the flavor to enhance your food, not to overpower it.

CAUTION: Never use evergreen wood such as pine or spruce for smoking, as your food will be saturated with resins. Only use hardwoods for smoking and grilling.

THE BEST WOODS TO USE FOR FLAVORING

- **Beef:** Hickory, oak, mesquite
- **Pork:** Alder, pecan, cherry, hickory, maple, mesquite
- **Lamb:** Apple, cherry, oak
- **Poultry:** Alder, apple, cherry, hickory, maple, mesquite, oak
- **Fish and shellfish:** Alder, hickory, mesquite, oak

WOOD FLAVORS

- **Oak:** Excellent for smoking large pieces of meat, such as brisket, for considerable lengths of time. Oak generally produces a medium to heavy (but not overpowering) flavor.
- **Hickory:** Known as the king of woods, this gives food a strong, sweet flavor. It is perfect for ribs and pork. ☞

- **Pecan:** This imparts a medium, fruity flavor and is good for briskets and pork roasts.
- **Apple:** Mild enough for chicken and turkey, apple has a mild, fruity flavor that makes meat taste slightly sweet. You could also use it to smoke a ham.
- **Alder:** With its light, delicate, mild flavor, alder is perfect for cooking poultry and is also the traditional wood to choose for smoking salmon.
- **Cherry:** Similar in flavor to apple, cherry has a mild, sweet, fruity flavor. It is extremely versatile, and you can use it for lamb, pork, ham, chicken and turkey.
- **Maple:** Mildly smoky, this goes well with poultry, ham, and vegetables, imparting a sweet and light taste.
- **Mesquite:** The flavor is strong and quickly transferred, so use this wood sparingly. The smoke should not penetrate the food.

If in doubt about whether your food has cooked through, cut it open with a sharp knife and check that it is done to your taste. However, do not be tempted to overcook meat in an effort to make it fall off the bone. This in itself does not necessarily indicate tenderness but can indicate meat that is dry and tough. Fire will burn your food, rather than cook it, giving it a nasty flavor, so keep the flames low!

Toasting Marshmallows

Toasting marshmallows over an open fire is a tradition that is almost as old as fire itself. Many people believe that the tradition dates back to ancient Rome while others think it dates to ancient Egypt.

Originally the marshmallow was made by scraping out the gooey center of the *Althaea officinalis* or marsh mallow plant and mixing it together with honey or sugar. And if you were around in France during the 1800s you would have enjoyed marshmallow as candy in all shapes and forms. This candy found its way to America early in the twentieth century. Progress came into play and the ingredients used in making marshmallows changed to incorporate things like gelatin and corn syrup in place of the original plant extract. But the fact is that marshmallows continue to be one of the most popular forms of confectionery there is, and campers love to bring out a bag the moment a campfire is lit.

Toasting a marshmallow couldn't be simpler. Take your marshmallow and stick it onto the end of a stick. Aim the stick, marshmallow end, toward the campfire and position yourself so that you can comfortably move your marshmallow in and out of the actual flames of the campfire. If you hold it away from the flame, it will eventually start to bubble slightly and turn a bit brown. But if you touch the flame, the marshmallow will catch alight (which is a good thing!). Control the burn by slowly turning the toasting stick. The marshmallow should be piping hot and will develop a warm and deliciously gooey inside. The exterior crust should be bittersweet, burnt, and sugary. Bite into your marshmallow very carefully so you don't burn your lips.

Try to picture the ancient Egyptians toasting marshmallows. Or the ancient Romans: "Friends, Romans, Countrymen... I come to Rome to toast marshmallows." Whoever it was that started the tradition, it's a pleasurable campfire treat that has remained popular and goes hand in hand with the whole camping experience.

S'mores

S'mores are one of the most popular campfire delicacies at summer camps all over the United States. Recipes for "Some Mores" appear in Girl Scout publications up until 1971, although it's unclear as to when the name was shortened to S'mores.

Who came up with the idea for S'mores? Was it the cowboys? Was it the pioneers? Or could it have been the Girl Scouts, who just so happen to have had the following recipe in their handbook, *Tramping and Trailing with the Girls Scouts*, (Girl Scouts of the USA, 1927)?

MAKES 8 SERVINGS

> 8 sticks for toasting the marshmallows
> 16 graham crackers
> 8 bars plain chocolate (broken in two)
> 16 marshmallows

Toast two marshmallows over the coals to a crisp gooey state and then put them inside a graham cracker and chocolate bar sandwich. The heat of the marshmallow between the halves of chocolate bar will melt the chocolate a bit. Though it tastes like "some more" one is really enough.

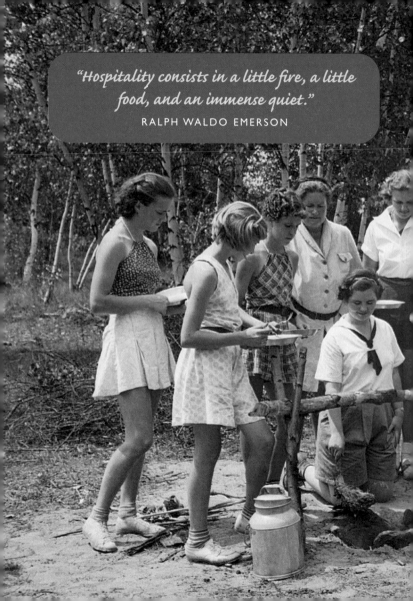

"Hospitality consists in a little fire, a little food, and an immense quiet."

RALPH WALDO EMERSON

Boy Scout Adventure

As Boy Scouts, we camped in the Canadian woods during the height of winter. Snow and ice abounded, and on our first night in a log cabin, we lay in our bedrolls watching as the silhouette of a curious grizzly bear played across the windows. Its alarming image was made even more dramatic by the flickering of the campfire flames outside, which illuminated the scene.

Our task, next morning, was to take with us the provisions we were issued, go out to a designated spot where we would each gather the fuel, and build and light a small campfire to cook our breakfasts. Needless to say, some ate and warmed themselves long before others did, but by the end of the experience we had all succeeded in freeing the fire from the wood and nobody went hungry. In fact, as luck or provenance would have it, the largest of the campfires soon became life-saving when one of our troopers fell through the ice on a riverbank and was rescued to be seated by the fire's warmth to dry out. I imagine that none of us present will ever forget the poor lad as he sat there with steam rising from him, glowing in the warmth of his friends and colleagues, savoring the nectar that is campfire hot chocolate, grateful for the warmth of the campfire.

One thing is certain though, that every one of us came away from the experience better for it and learned that under any circumstances we have the ability to make a fire.

Letters Home

One constant of camp life, particularly military camp life, has been mail call. It's that time when letters between loved ones caught up with each other, closing the distance between them, for a brief few moments. Mail call provides those unfortunate displaced soldiers a link with their homelife and a glimpse of another time, another place far from the horrors and reality of war. It is remarkable to think of all the places that letters have reached at times of civil disruption, the frontline trenches of World War II and the American Civil War. Letters that arrived in camp came as a breath of fresh air and played an important part in keeping up the morale of the recipients. The letters were often filled with hometown gossip and mixed news.

The call that everyone heard throughout camp and responded to was an NCO shouting out, "Mail Call!" Even the most exhausted soldier would rally in the hope of having his name called out and an envelope passed to him. It's still the same today. Camp is one place where there is time to think, to reflect, and to get one's thoughts down in words and send them off in hope of reaching those left behind. Filled perhaps with reassuring words and news, they are always penned with that awful thought in the back of one's mind that these might be the last words, the final sentiments. It makes for some exceedingly poignant correspondence and every generation can learn a great deal from the letters of another. There are the hysterical epistles expounding the shortfalls of mess hall cooks at boot camp. Some are highly romantic letters, as young lovers struggle to keep their relationships on the boil. If there is one enduring image of the soldier at camp, it is of him reading a letter from, or writing a letter to, his home.

Home on the Range

BY JOHN A. LOMAX (ORIGINAL TEXT BY BREWSTER HIGLEY)

Oh give me a home where the buffalo roam,
Where the deer and the antelope play,
Where seldom is heard a discouraging word,
And the skies are not cloudy all day.

CHORUS
Home, home on the range,
Where the deer and the antelope play,
Where seldom is heard a discouraging word,
And the skies are not cloudy all day.

Where the air is so pure, and the zephyrs so free,
The breezes so balmy and light,
That I would not exchange my home on the range,
For all of the cities so bright.
CHORUS

The red man was pressed from this part of the west,
He's likely no more to return,
To the banks of the Red River where seldom if ever
Their flickering campfires burn.
CHORUS

How often at night when the heavens are bright,
With the light from the glittering stars,
Have I stood there amazed and asked as I gazed,
If their glory exceeds that of ours.

CHORUS

Oh, I love these wild flowers in this dear land of ours,
The curlew I love to hear cry,
And I love the white rocks and the antelope flocks,
That graze on the mountain slopes high.

CHORUS

Oh give me a land where the bright diamond sand,
Flows leisurely down in the stream;
Where the graceful white swan goes gliding along,
Like a maid in a heavenly dream.

CHORUS

Then I would not exchange my home on the range,
Where the deer and the antelope play;
Where seldom is heard a discouraging word,
And the skies are not cloudy all day.

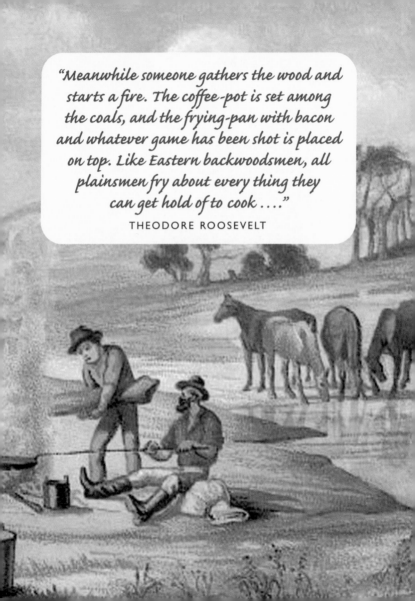

"Meanwhile someone gathers the wood and starts a fire. The coffee-pot is set among the coals, and the frying-pan with bacon and whatever game has been shot is placed on top. Like Eastern backwoodsmen, all plainsmen fry about every thing they can get hold of to cook ...."

THEODORE ROOSEVELT

How To Fish

There is nothing like sitting down at the campfire to watch,
listen to, smell, and taste the fish you caught earlier that day.
Sizzling over an open flame, whetting your appetite, you relive
the moment of their capture. The meal takes on an entirely
new meaning when you have caught, prepared, and cooked
the fish yourself. It is also a valuable source of food containing
good protein, vitamins, and fats. It's pretty safe to presume that
any freshwater fish you catch are edible (apart from piranha
or electric eels). If in doubt, invest in a book or study up
before going fishing.

People tend to worry unduly about their ability to catch
fish using conventional methods, but when you come to
understand a bit about feeding habits you can almost
guarantee success. Get to know the places fish tend to
congregate for feeding and sheltering. These spots will change
according to the times of the day, the climate of the weather,
or the range of the temperatures.

Fish tend to seek out sheltered places such as submerged
logs or rocks, or they hide under riverbank ledges to meditate
when the river is in flood or fast-flowing. They sometimes lurk
at the outside of a bend or stay tucked away in the comparative
stillness of small tributaries that lead off the main flow. When it
is cold and sunny, fish prefer the shallows where it feels a little
warmer or they tend to congregate around the edges of lakes.

The opposite is true when it is very hot. Then they tend to prefer deep shaded pools in rivers or the deeper, cooler parts of a lake.

It's probably a waste of time to attempt fishing after a heavy rainstorm, but excellent practice to fish just before one breaks as the fish tend to grab all of the food they can get at the surface, as if they know what's coming. Many campers prefer to fish at night. Sleep during the day and take advantage of the moonlight that fish love, or, if in a survival situation, leave out some night lines that can be checked just before morning light breaks.

The basic rule of thumb is that when you want to catch larger fish, use a larger hook. But the best way to catch both large and smaller fish is with a fairly small hook. (If you're starving and have no hooks, you can improvise one from thorns, bone, bent pins, or even whittled wood.) However, always bear in mind that fish can, because of the image refraction on the water, see quite a bit of what's happening on the bank side. So stand far back and remain as still and patient as possible, and the effort will pay off with a fresh catch of fish that you can either dry, smoke, fry, cook on a stick, bake in a Dutch oven, simmer in a soup, cook on hot coals, or steam.

Experiment with floats and weights, and soon you'll be able to take your hook to exactly where the fish are biting.

"More than half the intense enjoyment of fly-fishing is derived from the beautiful surroundings, the satisfaction felt from being in the open air, the new lease of life secured thereby, and the many, many pleasant recollections of all one has seen, heard, and done."

CHARLES F. ORVIS

Fish Hooks

With some line and a hook and a good stretch of water, dinner is in the bag.

But in order to get those fish biting, you will first need to know a couple of basics about tying fishing knots. Here are a few tips that may help someday.

In the event you are stranded and have no nylon line or anything else, then gut can be used, but it must firstly be well soaked in water to make it pliable.

GUT LINE
For a gut line, the following knot called the Turtle knot should be used.

After you have soaked the gut, thread it through the eye of your fish hook. Make an overhand loop, and then pass a bight through it.
(See fig. 1)

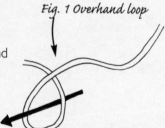

Fig. 1 Overhand loop

This will result in
a simple slip knot.
(See fig. 2)

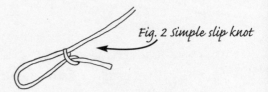

Fig. 2 Simple slip knot

Fig. 3 Pass hook through loop

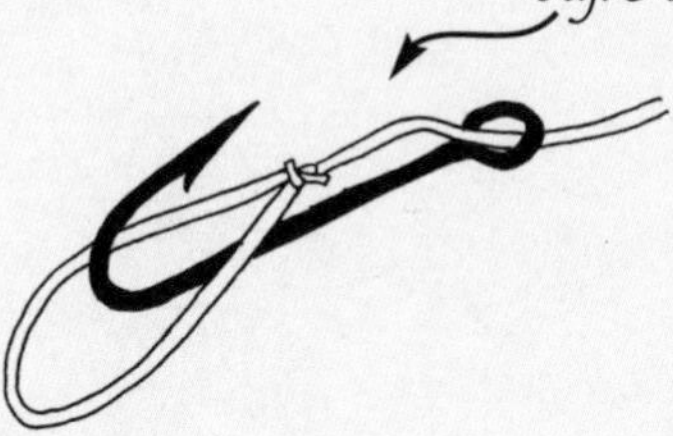

Next pass the hook
through
the loop of the slip knot.
(See fig. 3)

Then pull tight until the loop
slips snugly around the shank.
(See fig. 4)

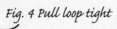

Fig. 4 Pull loop tight

NYLON LINE

It is also more likely that you will already have or be able to locate nylon fishing line. Nylon line needs a different knot. Nylon against itself has little grip, so the knot must be very effective and not slip. The best knot for the job is called the Blood Knot.

Thread the end of the line through the eye of the fish hook. Then make four turns around the trailing or standing part before passing the threaded end or live end through the loop that has been formed right next to the hook. (See fig. A)

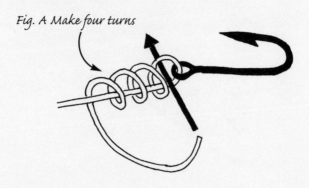

Fig. A Make four turns

Now pull the end until the knot is very taut, and then trim the end quite close to the hook. (See fig. B)

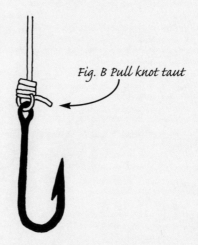

Fig. B Pull knot taut

Neither method is very difficult to achieve. It just takes a little practice, and soon you'll be pulling fish out of the water to grill on your campfire to the delight of your camping party.

Happy fishing!

"Everybody needs beauty as well as bread, places to play in and pray in, where nature may heal and cheer and give strength to body and soul alike."

JOHN MUIR

Family Camping

Camping is the perfect family pastime. What better way of bonding could there be than to share nights out sleeping under canvas, chatting by the campfire, communing with nature, and living off the fruits of the land? Parents and children can hike and fish together, each depending on the other, while parents pass on techniques that were handed down from the generation before.

There is a great deal of truth in the old saying, "The family that plays together stays together." The technology that pervades society today is designed primarily for solo indulgence and can drive wedges between family members. Conversely, camping demands interaction, understanding, and team spirit, whether it's pitching a tent, cooking a meal, paddling a canoe, or helping to reel in a fish. By its very nature camping poses questions that require answers and often provokes debate. Practicality is the deciding factor that gives each family member an equal voice and position of relevance in the scheme of things. It's a wonderful time to get to know each other away from the demands and constraints of everyday life with its pressures and timetabling. These days, families are lucky if they even see each other more than a few hours a week, so it's little wonder that rifts develop. A family camping vacation brings people back together and leads to a greater understanding of each others needs, wants, and aspirations. There are plenty of people coming back from vacations complaining about the quality of the service or facilities at their hotel. Then there's lost baggage, delayed flights, noisy discos, and the list goes on. Ask a family who have just returned from a camping vacation how it all went, and they'll tell you it was great!

Picture Credits